Owning
ITIL®

a skeptical guide
for decision-makers

Rob England

(The IT Skeptic)

Sensible business practices

Created by Two Hills Ltd

letterbox@twohills.co.nz

www.twohills.co.nz

PO Box 57-150, Mana
Porirua 5247
New Zealand

Published by Two Hills
First published 2009

ISBN-10: 0958296901

ISBN-13: 978-0-9582969-0-8

This book is essential reading for **all decision makers** (IT-literate or not) who are presented with an ITIL® proposal or asked to oversee an ITIL project, or who find something called "ITIL" or "Service Management" in their budget. It tells you what the ITIL industry won't.

For **everyone else involved in ITIL** projects, read this book to help you stay grounded and safe.

Every IT department in the world is at least pondering ITIL. As the ITIL projects proliferate, **this book is for the executives who must fund them or manage them, and for those who ask those executives for money**. The book explains, in lay-manager's terms, **what ITIL is**. It reveals what ITIL is **good** for, what it is **bad** at, what to **expect** from it. It describes how to ensure an ITIL project **succeeds**, what to look for in the **business case**, and how to measure the **results**.

It does these things **in business terms**, written by an **independent and critical observer**. Read the book to get an understanding of ITIL and a context for the recommendations. Or just read the 101 recommendations which have been picked out for your convenience. The busiest managers can use the four checklists at the back as ITIL survival tools.

Cover: Toi toi against a forest of black beech, Kaitoke (a.k.a. "Rivendell"), New Zealand. Photos by the author.

Dedicated to Art Jacobs, the man who turned the business light on for this geek.

The Community of ITIL Owners

There is a community of readers of this book at the Owning ITIL website at www.itskeptic.org/owningitil. There you can find

- additional material

- readers' discussions

- updates and corrections to the book

About the recommendations

In many places in this book I provide specific recommendations.

These recommendations will be discussed on the Owning ITIL website at www.itskeptic.org/owningitil, where they will be subject to debate and development. Please check in to see if and how they have changed.

Contents

Preface

Some will suggest that it is ungrateful of me to bite the hand that feeds me. ITIL was a key part of my income in the past and it still tops up the exchequer through a little local consulting.

I would respond that as a devout skeptic[1], it behoves me to point out fuzzy thinking wherever I find it, not least in my professional environment.

Now that ITIL is the de facto standard for IT operations, the time is ripe for a more objective evaluation of ITIL's merits and caveats. In the ITIL world it is still spring or summer. This book seeks to balance that with an icy blast of winter through the techniques of the skeptic – consider the observable facts and question the underlying assumptions – as well as applying that other great Litmus test: common sense[2].

There are more words than I would have liked but I want to leave you equipped to deal with everything you will encounter out there. The book does repeat a few points, for two reasons: first, to reinforce them; and second, because not everyone will read it from cover to cover.

Along the way I offer advice and recommendations. Some of these may be blindingly obvious to you. Please excuse me and do not take them as patronising. I have met all levels of

---

[1] Modern skeptics like to spell skeptic with a "k" to differentiate from the colloquial meaning and negative connotation that have become associated with "sceptic".

[2] Common sense is something that used to be common, hence the name. You youngsters can look it up on Wikipedia.

managers in my career so far and I have tried to write for all of them.

This is not a negative book. We discuss the benefits of ITIL and how to succeed in an ITIL transformation (this book explains why that is a better word than "implementation"). It simply seeks to bring some balance to ITIL considerations. The assertions made here are debatable and that is my intent: to engender some much needed debate around common assumptions. ITIL is not a silver bullet: the decision to invest in it should be a considered one. I certainly believe there is a vacuum that this book fills: independent analysis of ITIL for those charged with governing it not doing it.

My fervent hope is that this book will decrease the number of ITIL projects but increase the number of successful ones. May you be a beneficiary of my success.

Let me extend my heartfelt thanks to everyone who contributed to, reviewed, and assisted with this book. In particular, thanks for invaluable feedback from Harvey Calder, James Finister, Cary A. King, and Paul Wilkinson.

A special thank-you is required to my loving wife and son who put up with all this.

Executive Summary

You don't need ITIL to run a static environment where nothing goes wrong and nothing changes and nothing grows. ITIL has nothing to do with technology, nor can it be implemented with technology. ITIL is about how an organisation and the people within it respond to planned and unexpected variations in the environment, from outages to changes to growth, in order to meet the needs of the business. ITIL defines human behaviour.

Every organisation needs the processes ITIL describes. Every organisation already has them. ITIL is just one way of defining a standard approach to performing them. You may not need ITIL but every IT shop needs to be doing what ITIL describes, one way or another.

Some ITIL initiatives should never see the light of day, or if they get that far they should be put out of their misery. The ITIL fad/hype/cult phenomenon creates proposals that are not an optimal use of resources.

ITIL appeals to the IT taste for instant product solutions to complex problems. It looks like a nicely packaged, formulaic fix to service-culture issues. It is not, but that has not stopped the vendor/consultant/analyst community from hyping it as such, and building consulting, training and software markets off the back of it.

There is a lot of nonsense spread about ITIL, such as: ITIL cannot be measured until you have put ITIL in to provide the metrics; ITIL needs a complex CMDB technology to make it work; ITIL cannot and should not be cost justified – you just need it.

There is nothing magic about ITIL: any project built around it should be justified and managed and held accountable in the same ways as any other.

If you find yourself owning an "ITIL" line item in your budget; if you have been assigned ownership of an ITIL project; if you are asked to approve a business case for something called ITIL; then this book speaks to you. Properly forewarned and enlightened about ITIL, you can make the right decisions. And if you **report** to one of those people, this book will help you to say and do the right things.

ITIL is a useful tool in the context of a broader cultural change initiative, to change the way people approach delivery of service. If there is a real need, and if there is a justifiable business case, then ITIL can usefully be employed as one input to culture change and process improvement, where it provides a template for generally agreed good practice. If ITIL is presented as more than this, or as an end in its own right, then this book will help you squash that. By focusing on only those initiatives that should happen, I hope more of them can succeed. Instead of – say - 3 out of 10 ITIL projects succeeding, I'd like to see us win 4 out of 7[1].

Look for the right reasons and mindset going into the project. Watch out for zealotry and scope creep during the project. Measure the results of the project and hold the advocates accountable. Ensure there is an ongoing activity to maintain the achievements of the project and to build on them.

---

[1] "From 3 out of 10 to 4 out of 7" is a concept that I learnt from Art Jacobs and the Target Account Selling methodology

Most of all, ITIL is about changing people: changing the way they think about IT, changing the way they work. If ITIL projects aren't focused on people change - if they are captured by the concerns of process and technology - they will fail.

For you to succeed your team should put most of their energy into changing the hearts and minds of people. From this will come a desire and capability to change the processes. From process change will come a definition of the needs for supporting technology. Never let the toys-oriented geeks who are inside your organisation - or the "out-of-the-box solution" software vendors outside it - try to drive that sequence backwards. Tools don't fix process and process won't change people.

The undertaking is a big one. Approach it as a real and serious project, with your genuine and visible executive commitment, with funding and dedicated resources. The learning curve is high: outside expertise is essential. At the same time, the consulting and vendor industry is as voracious and predatory as any in IT, so manage them closely. Manage it as real project in the usual way meeting all the usual criteria, and ITIL can make a real improvement to the way IT delivers service to your customers.

There is a frenzy surrounding ITIL at the moment. There is a lot of irrational activity, which equates to financial inefficiency. The inefficiency survives because of the mystical nature of ITIL. This book attempts to remove some of that mystery for those owning and managing ITIL. It is up to you as the governors and managers of ITIL to restore rationality for the sake of your organisations... and your careers.

About ITIL

The IT world is traditionally split into systems and operations halves (or you may call it solutions and delivery, or development and production). In the operations hemisphere, ITIL has been the centre of attention for all of this millennium. If you aren't familiar with ITIL, you should read this chapter, if only to be in the know at those awful parties where people talk IT like a secret language. If you are familiar, you might find some new perspectives in here.

What is ITIL

ITIL is - depending on your perspective - either a set of books for sale, or a worldwide movement sweeping the IT community. ITIL is a creation of the Office of Government Commerce (OGC), a British Government body. Actually it was created by a more IT-centric predecessor of the OGC in the 1980s but this is not the place for an ITIL history lesson. According to the OGC[1]

> "ITIL® (the IT Infrastructure Library) is the most widely accepted approach to IT service management in the world. ITIL® provides a cohesive set of best practice, drawn from the public and private sectors internationally. It is supported by a comprehensive qualifications scheme, accredited training organisations, and implementation and assessment tools. The best practice processes promoted in ITIL® support and are supported by, the British Standards Institution's standard for IT service Management (BS15000)" [and now BS15000 is superseded by ISO/IEC 20000].

This is a modest description. ITIL is the most widely accepted approach to *IT management* in the world. Theoretically service management is only one way to approach the job of managing IT operations, but no-one has come up with a better one yet. Service Management seeks to align IT with the business, a fancy way of saying they give the business what it needs not what IT wants to give it. This is just what everyone is trying to do these days, and ITIL is the best compilation of documentation, a "body of knowledge", on how to do that. It has been around for years but its time has come.

The number one benefit unique to ITIL is undoubtedly standardisation, a lingua franca. Auditors, consultants,

---

[1] www.ogc.gov.uk/guidance_itil.asp

service providers and new staff can quickly understand what is what and who is who if you use standard ITIL terms (and use them in the standard way). ITIL is the de facto standard language for IT operations.

The second benefit is the momentum of ITIL. Trained people, experienced consultants, good books, internet content, forums and other resources are widely available. By attaching the ITIL handle to a service culture initiative, it can help get approval and funding [...or not, depending on the baggage carried by the approvers: sometimes it is better not to call it ITIL].

There are other benefits that are not unique to ITIL:

- a focus on a service-oriented culture/mindset

- a framework to check oneself against. What are we missing? What are we doing OK?

- a certification program for practitioners

- a catalyst for cultural change and process reengineering

- some raw material to get you started in designing improved processes and roles

On the other hand, ITIL has become something of a cult. That is, objectivity goes out the window. We follow the holy books, we do it because ITIL says so not because we have a business case, we do it the ITIL way not the best way, we will review all our processes not just the ones that are broken, ITIL for its own sake. As a result, ITIL projects can over-engineer and fix things that are not broken: i.e. they can be a poor use of funds.

Secondly, ITIL has become captive of commercial interests - something that was inevitable once it reached a certain size and momentum. This means ITIL does not always develop in the best interests of the end user/consumers who are poorly represented, nor of the overall advancement of the service management philosophy.

Finally, ITIL is aloof; it integrates badly with other important systems such as COBIT[1], ISO2700x, ISO900x, and CMMI; even the integration with ISO20000[2] is loose. The result is greater costs in bringing these systems together within an organization.

Overall though, ITIL provides a positive benefit to IT where appropriately and properly applied.

Although COBIT in many ways appears a more comprehensive and reliable body of knowledge, ITIL is more popular. The IT Skeptic draws this analogy: ITIL is the hitchhiker's guide, COBIT is the encyclopaedia, rather like the fictional books the *Hitch Hiker's Guide to the Galaxy* and the *Encyclopedia Galactica*.

That truly astonishing book, *The Hitchhiker's Guide to the Galaxy*[3] describes the fictional *Hitchhiker's Guide* book thus:

> In many of the more relaxed civilizations on the Outer Eastern Rim of the Galaxy, the Hitch Hiker's Guide has already supplanted the great Encyclopedia Galactica as the standard repository of all knowledge and wisdom, for though it has many omissions and contains much that is apocryphal, or at least wildly inaccurate, it scores over the older more pedestrian work in two important respects.

---

[1] *COBIT 4.0*, IT Governance Institute, 2005, ISBN 1-933284-37-4
www.isaca.org/AMTemplate.cfm?Section=Overview&Template=/ContentManagement/ContentDisplay.cfm&ContentID=22940
[2] ISO20000 is the International Standards Organisation standard for IT Service Management. It is more correctly called ISO/IEC 20000 but almost noone does.
[3] *The Hitchhiker's Guide to the Galaxy*, Douglas Adams, various publishers including Del Rey 1995, ISBN-13: 978-0345391803

> First, it is slightly cheaper: and secondly it has the words DON'T PANIC inscribed in large friendly letters on its cover."

Apart from the fact that ITIL is more expensive and it has large x-rays of plants and animals on the covers, Douglas Adams could be speaking about ITIL and COBIT.

ITIL is relaxed to the verge of sloppy (e.g. the use of the term "process").

ITIL is boisterous to the point of controversial (*Service Strategy* on value networks).

ITIL has many omissions compared to COBIT. ITIL focuses on operations, and mostly ignores development/solutions. ITIL seldom ventures into project management or portfolio management, and it skips a lot of aspects of request management.

Most of all, COBIT systematically chronicles a checklist of all the things we ought to be doing, and their properties, but ITIL explains how.

> Here's what the Encyclopedia Galactica has to say about alcohol. It says that alcohol is a colourless volatile liquid formed by the fermentation of sugars and also notes its intoxicating effect on certain carbon-based life forms.
>
> The Hitch Hiker's Guide also mentions alcohol. It says that the best drink in existence is the Pan Galactic Gargle Blaster.
>
> It says that the effect of a Pan Galactic Gargle Blaster is like having your brains smashed out by a slice of lemon wrapped round a large gold brick.
>
> The Guide also tells you on which planets the best Pan Galactic Gargle Blasters are mixed, how much you can expect to pay for one and what voluntary organizations exist to help you rehabilitate afterwards.

> The Guide even tells you how you can mix one
> yourself...
>
> The Hitch Hiker's Guide to the Galaxy sells rather
> better than the Encyclopedia Galactica.

It is remarkable the correlation with ITIL and COBIT.

An encyclopaedic entry recording the existence of a chemical called alcohol is of considerably less interest than a practical guide to the preparation, imbibing and recovery from the universe's best drink. The fact that the *Hitchhiker's Guide* is incomplete, out-of-date, opinionated and unreliable is far outweighed by its usefulness and practicality... and humanness. Its fallibility and quirkiness is part of the attraction. So it is with ITIL.

ITIL books

The tangible part of ITIL is a set of books.

There are several versions of ITIL. In 2007, Version 2 (in this book "ITIL2") was "refreshed" by the new Version 3 ("ITIL3").

ITIL1 is still in print and there are those (a dwindling band of diehards) who swear by the original Version 1 books.

Core

There are a number of **core** books (about nine or ten in ITIL2, five or six in ITIL3 – depending on who is counting) that are the "official" set. These describe the processes that are the "best" way of doing IT operations. They go into a detail about roles of people, activities to be performed, how the processes link together, and so on.

In ITIL2 there was even a "core within the core". Many people mistakenly think that there were only two ITIL2 books: the "red book" *Service Delivery*[1] and the "blue book" *Service Support*[2].

Contrary to popular belief, ITIL is not in the public domain. The books are copyright the OGC, published by the British Government Stationary Office (TSO), now TSO a private for-profit company. Copyright is owned by Her Majesty the Queen (though I doubt she has read them). The trademark is defended by OGC – well, so they say although there are a large number of products using the ITIL name without license.

---

[1] *Service Delivery*, OGC, TSO 2001, ISBN 978-0113300174
[2] *Service Support*, CCTA, TSO 2000, ISBN 978-0113300150

The books can be bought as old-fashioned books, or as single- or multi-user CDs (ITIL2) or e-books (.pdfs) and online subscriptions (ITIL3).

ITIL books are not cheap.

The minimum ITIL2 set of "the blue book and the red book" will set you back a cool six hundred bucks on CD ROM or half that on paper. The other books tend to run to about the same or a few for about half that much each. So a full set of ITIL2 would not leave much change out of a thousand British pounds on CD or a thousand US dollars on paper.

The main five ITIL3 books can be had as a set for three hundred pounds. Alternatively you can take out a single user annual subscription to ITIL3 for about the same price as the hardcopy books are to buy outright, and corporate online licences are open for negotiation. This is still less than some of the proprietary frameworks and methodologies peddled by consulting firms, but certainly more than the free open content emerging from the Internet MOF, COBIT and FITS (see p34) are all free.

In addition, *The Official Introduction to the ITIL Service Lifecycle*[1] is often treated as the sixth core ITIL3 book.

Books can be obtained from

- TSO the publisher, www.tsoshop.co.uk

- Van Haren, www.vanharen.net

- Amazon, www.amazon.com

- Many other online shops

- Your itSMF local chapter

---

[1] *The Official Introduction to the ITIL Service Lifecycle*, OGC, TSO 2007, ISBN 978-0113310616

- itSMF International (especially if you arc an itSMF Global Member you will get a better deal internationally than from your local chapter, which does not make the local chapters happy)

Complementary

Then there are **complementary** books that provide supplementary advice and different perspectives. A popular example is the ITIL2 introductory pocketbook on ITIL[1]. They are published by a number of sources, and tend to be priced more like typical business books.

In ITIL3 there are official Complementary books approved and integrated with the core, as distinct from third party publications such as this one you are reading. The first Complementary book is *Passing your ITIL Foundation Exam*[2], and the second is *Building an ITIL based Service Management Department*[3] (about organisational structure, not about the process of getting to ITIL). Coming in 2009 is *Delivering IT Services using ITIL, PRINCE2 and DSDM Atern* (DSDM Atern is not an Irish soldier: it is an obscure methodology that everyone is pretending they had already heard of).

itSMF International has the contract from OGC to produce an ongoing series of translations of ITIL3 into a wide range of languages.

Also considered part of the ITIL3 Complementary Publications is the ITIL Live™ portal[4], a website owned, operated and copyrighted by TSO as a commercial

---

[1] *An Introductory Overview of ITIL*, Rudd, itSMF, 2004
[2] *Passing your ITIL foundation exam: the official study aid*, Nissen, TSO, 2007, ISBN 978-0113310791
[3] *Building an ITIL based Service Management Department*, M. Fry, TSO 2008, ISBN 9780113310968
[4] www.bestpracticelive.com

enterprise. And it shows, with individual subscriptions costing £2500 and concurrent commercial user subscriptions costing twice that. What the value is and whether anyone will pay these prices remains to be seen.

Worth a look are the "alternate" ITIL books, not considered officially Complementary, owned by itSMF International and published by van Haren, known as the ITSM Library. Especially notable is *Foundations of IT Service Management Based on ITIL V3*[1]which is an excellent in-depth coverage (not summary) of the five ITIL core books, but without all the duplication and fragmentation.

Finally there are a lot of third party ITIL books such as this one. Look on Amazon.

Recommendations

1. When starting out with ITIL it is worth reading about ITIL3 to get the big picture even if you then head down the ITIL2 road.

2. For your first book to read consider buying *Passing your ITIL Foundation Exam*. When compared with the more obvious place to start, *The Official Introduction to the ITIL Service Lifecycle*, it is the same size, half the price, and covers much the same territory. And it includes sample exam questions to check whether you are actually getting the hang of it or not. [Note: as of early 2009 this book was out of date due to the ongoing changes to the ITIL V3 Foundation syllabus. The book still makes a great introduction but we do **not** recommend it as a study guide for the exam unless it is revised.]

---

[1] *Foundations of IT Service Management based on ITIL V3*, van Bon (editor), van Haren 2005, ISBN 978-9077212585

3. The *Foundation Exam* study guide may prove to be all you need. If you need more, read *The Official Introduction*. Alternatively, if you are really on a budget, or if all you want to do is talk the talk, then read itSMF's free download *An Introductory Overview of ITIL V3*[1].

4. An "owner" of ITIL is unlikely to need any more, but you could consider an ITIL Foundation training course.

5. If that isn't enough, then read one of either the ITIL2 "red book and blue book set" (*Service Support* and *Service Delivery*) or *Foundations of IT Service Management based on ITIL V3*.

6. If you need to read the five ITIL3 core books, you have too much time on your hands for a decision maker.

---

[1] *An Introductory Overview of ITIL V3*, itSMF 2007, ISBN 0-9551245-8-1 www.itsmfi.org/files/itSMF_ITILV3_Intro_Overview.pdf

ITIL movement

ITIL started out as just the books, but it is much more today: it is a movement, a professional group, and an industry.

A great deal of activity goes on in promotion and support of ITIL worldwide. Much of it is ungoverned and ad-hoc. There are many pillars of the house of ITIL and OGC governs and manages only four.

Core content

Owned by OGC and tightly controlled through copyright. Good stuff.

Individual certification

Other than the content, certification is the other Pillar of ITIL that OGC did well: establishing the ITIL Certification Management Board (ICMB) and accrediting the trainers and examiners. In late 2006, OGC outsourced accreditation and examination of ITIL to a private company, APM Group or APMG.

Brand

The ITIL brand is wrapped up by registered trademark in the UK and USA.

Complementary content

The official complementary publications are well regulated and quality assured. The independent – and hence unregulated - ITIL book industry (of which this book is an example) is of course a mixed bag – they are not all as good as this one.

Governing body

There isn't one. There is no über-body that represents all the stakeholders, has elected members, sets policy and strategy, and provides governance for all the Pillars of ITIL. As one vendor says[1] "The ITIL market is still predominantly a market guided by customers but dependent on a delicate coalition of interests (OGC, itSMF, APMG, ISO, TSO, EXIN, ISEB, education companies, consulting companies, and tool suppliers). For the market to work effectively, the players need to collaborate."

The Combined Strategy Board (CSB), chaired by OGC, does not provide this function. APMG says[2] the Board has "responsibility for global marketing and overall product development" which is a promotional role rather than governance one. Moreover there is no transparency of this body: it publishes little, its membership is appointed not elected, and it has no accountability.

Professional body

There was nothing until recently that provided registration or a college for practicing professionals. Now we have the Institute of Service Management in the UK and the Institute of Certified Service Managers in the USA. Or the ITSM Institute. Or the Service Management Society. Or the IT Infrastructure Management Association. Or the Association for Services Management International. Or the AITP or IEEE or ... None of these have the official recognition or charter of OGC, and OGC provides no governance over their activities or standards.

---

[1] *Perspectives on the Developments around ITIL-3 and Accreditation,* ITpreneurs,
itpreneurs.com/Content/Resources/Trends/itil/itil-3_and_accreditation.htm
[2] *International Best Practice for IT Service Management*
www.apmgroup.co.uk/nmsruntime/saveasdialog.asp?lID=532&sID=222

User group

The itSMF, the IT Service Management Forum[1], arose from ITIL and regards itself as the unofficial guardian of the "integrity" of ITIL (although the OGC is not consistent in seeing it that way). It is often presumed to be the user group for ITIL practitioners and users. But it isn't. According to its aims, itSMF is a body dedicated to the promotion of service management standards and practices, including ITIL. itSMF's purpose is to promote the service management industry not the interests of the user community (unless they happen to coincide).

In practice it varies from country to country: in some itSMF is an ITIL networking club; in others it is the public face of ITIL, serving the theoretical aims; in others it veers close to being the captive body of vendors. Sometimes it presents itself as the voice of members, but how does it derive its understanding of what members want? There is now an official online forum[2], but feedback mechanisms into OGC or itSMF are primitive or nonexistent. There is no voting, no surveys. Try suggesting additional or better content for a book. It would be more accurate to say itSMF represents the voice of the senior network of the ITIL "elite".

OGC has done nothing to create or control a community of ITIL practitioners and users. We hope it will one day address the whole issue of creating an online community and embracing 21st century collective technologies.

Industry regulation and governance

There is no control over the ITIL industry other than exam certification of trainers. When vendors of products or services are given the right to use the trademarked term

---

[1] www.itsmf.org
[2] www.itsmfi-forum.org

ITIL, no body governs what they do to ensure they do not misrepresent the concepts of ITIL or their capabilities to deliver them. In theory it is OGC, but there is no mechanism to effect this in practice.

Product certification

One of the leading ITIL consulting firms, Pink Elephant (a brand-name nobody forgets) stepped up to provide PinkVerify™ as a commercial offering to certify ITIL products because OGC consciously backed away from the whole issue of product certification.

Nor does ISO20000 appear to address it (yet – there are rumours of a "part four" that will).

There needs to be an open transparent non-commercial product certification mechanism run by an independent body and we needed it about ten years ago. The OGC/APMG "swirl" certification may provide this, but there are no published criteria and zero uptake.

APMG sell a service on behalf of OGC to authorise use of the OGC "swirl" logo (which encompasses all OGC best practice, not just ITIL), but no ITIL vendors are licensed as of end of 2008.

Organisational certification

In the absence of anything from OGC, the world's many consulting firms all had to (re-)invent their own ITIL maturity measurement methods and scales for assessing where their clients are at.

ITIL emphasises the Deming Cycle[1], and assessing As-Is status. But it provides no standard mechanism to measure ITIL status within an organisation. ITIL refers to CMM maturity levels but provides no guidance as to how to assess them. This was forgivable in the first version. It has been an obvious crying need ever since.

A standard

We waited a long time for BS15000, and now ISO20000, service management standard. An ITIL standard would have addressed the organisational certification issue and possibly the product one too, and given ITIL additional credibility in business. The result is that BS15000 and now ISO20000 came out so long after ITIL2 that the evolution of the industry meant the new standards are well in advance of what is in ITIL2[2].

We all hoped that ITIL3 would bring them back closer. While ISO20000, (and other important bodies of knowledge such as COBIT), are acknowledged in the ITIL3 books, there has been no systematic work done in the books to bring them all into alignment, or even to point out the links along the way, and ITIL3 persists in going its own way. Whilst the two have drawn closer there is still a gap[3]. There are extensions to ITIL and some differences:

- ISO20000 only recognises the management of financial assets, not assets which include "management, organization, process, knowledge, people, information, applications, infrastructure and financial capital", nor the concept of a "service asset". So ISO20000

---

[1] The Deming Cycle is a quality improvement process based on four steps - Plan, Do, Check, Act - performed cyclically.

[2] *ISO/IEC 20000 and ITIL - the difference explained*, J. Dugmore and A. Holt www.best-management-practice.com/bookstore.asp?FO=1229332&DI=571307

[3] *ITIL® V3 and ISO/IEC 20000*, J. Dugmore and S. Taylor, www.best-management-practice.com/gempdf/ITIL_and_ISO_20000_March08.pdf

certification says nothing about the management of 'assets' in an ITIL sense.

- ISO20000 does not recognise CMS or SKMS, and so does not certify anything beyond CMDB

- An organisation can obtain ISO20000 certification without recognising or implementing the ITIL concept of Known Error, usually considered essential ITIL.

The theorists offer the rationale that ITIL is not absolute (it is only guidance: "adopt and adapt") so there cannot be a standard, and/or that following a standard would constrain ITIL somehow. The fact that just about every consulting vendor manages to define their own assessment "standard" undermines this argument.

ITIL industry

ITIL is the books and the books are ITIL, but there is an ITIL industry surrounding the books. That industry now runs into the billions of dollars per annum, so it has the attention of many players.

itSMF

The itSMF is non-profit, but does very nicely from memberships, conferences and its own complementary publications. There are chapters in over 50 countries[1].

Membership is useful for at least the key ITIL people from your organisation. You can buy transferable multi-seat corporate memberships in each country, or a global membership.

Vendors of software

ITIL does not mandate software, but a service desk tool is pretty much essential, so the service desk vendors are all keen on ITIL.

The vendors have convinced the community that CMDB and other service management tools are equally essential.

ITIL also drives demand for other IT operations tools for monitoring, alerting, discovering, auditing, managing, reporting and so on.

ITIL is big business for many software vendors: big firms such as HP and IBM, service management tool vendors like CA and BMC, and niche vendors like Marval and Service-Now. Microsoft, Oracle, Novell and others are entering the market. There are far too many to list in full.

---

[1] http://www.itsmfi.org/content/chapters

Consulting

Consultants are an essential element of any successful ITIL implementation. There is no quicker or more cost effective way to inject ITIL knowledge into your organisation. It comes pre-digested, already over the learning hump, and customised to your requirements.

The trick, like any engagement of consultants, is to find good ones and keep them in check. There are four main types:

- the big consulting firms (Accenture co-authored one of the ITIL3 books)

- the ITSM consulting specialists, such as Pink Elephant (most other big specialists are regional)

- the vendors. Beware of the "box droppers" who are product only and have little or no consulting services

- the independents, people who usually have an ITIL Expert certification and a few big implementations on their CV

Training and Certification

Although many of the consultants are also trainers, this is a separate industry in its own right.

There is no OGC-ratified certification of organisations or software in ITIL, but there is definitely certification of individuals and accreditation of trainers and training organisations.

The basic certificate is the ITIL Foundation. A large proportion of staff get ITIL Foundation certificate as part of many ITIL implementations. This is referred to as "sheep dipping". It is often overdone, but it does produce a few zealous project supporters.

There are a number of ITIL Intermediate (called Practitioner's in ITIL2) certificates to train specific ITIL roles in the organisation.

An ITIL Expert (previously ITIL Manager's or Master's) certificate is currently the top qualification.

A higher ITIL3 Advanced level of qualification, confusingly now called an ITIL Master's, is under development.

All of these qualifications provide a useful indicator of basic knowledge, but be aware that they are based on a few days or at most a week or two of training, followed by a multiple-choice exam. They require no practical experience, no practical or written examination, no peer review, no ongoing professional development, no re-certification, and certainly do not include the level of study of a tertiary degree.

As mentioned, the accreditation of ITIL examination bodies and trainers has been outsourced by the OGC to a private company, APMG.

Some vendors offer simulations as part of their training, often as an adjunct to ITIL Foundation. These are a highly effective mechanism for helping people rapidly get it - learning by doing. They are worth taking standalone.

Publishing

The core books and some official complementary books, as well as the translations, are published by TSO (The Stationery Office) which was a function of her Majesty's British Government until sold off in 2006, and since re-sold.

There are a number of other publishers as well, including itSMF and Van Haren.

The ITIL hype

Jaded observers of IT could be forgiven for wondering if ITIL is "just another Y2K". There certainly are some strong similarities.

Y2K became an industry in its own right. As momentum gathers, that very momentum becomes a powerful selling tool that few can resist. If you can't see some consulting firms and software vendors fanning the ITIL flames you need to stand back and look again.

The Y2K industry raised the art of FUD[1] to heights not seen before. Nor are we likely to see them again, as the world is wiser and more cynical as a result... one hopes (watch what vendors do with the recession of 2009). They whipped the business world into a frenzy of spending. Everyone did it because everyone else was doing it. You were mad if you didn't. Worse, you were negligent.

Does ITIL feed on FUD? No, but it feeds on the implicit assumption that everyone should do ITIL because everyone else is. Is it a bandwagon? Absolutely. Are the vendors and consultants jumping on? For sure. It has become an industry, and the industry's marketers learned a few techniques from Y2K for creating momentum.

So there are some interesting parallels with the Y2K phenomenon: the wave, the marketing frenzy, the "why aren't you?" mentality. Hopefully we have learnt something from Y2K so as not to repeat our mistakes. Hopefully we have learnt not to get stampeded into anything.

---

[1] Fear, Uncertainty and Doubt: a sales technique reportedly pioneered by IBM

Gartner[1] has a most useful model for considering the waves of irrational exuberance that regularly sweep across the IT industry: the hype cycle[2]: a peak of enthusiasm followed by a trough as reality sets in, then rising to a steady state.

The reality of most hype cycles is that the phenomenon in question settles down to a sedate middle age and eventually fades away from view (but in IT things seldom becomes obsolete, just another layer of complexity to be paid for and managed), while a new kid in town takes all the focus and glory.

ITIL is somewhere around the peak, though it varies around the world. It is not in the trough yet anywhere: it is still greeted with acclaim and enthusiasm and often inflated expectations. But progress down the slippery slope is beginning. Hopefully a little objectivity now can reduce the height of the peak and the depth of the trough, and ease the transition into a more stable maturity.

The IT industry is certainly prone to its fads. This is a reflection of the immaturity of the whole industry (as compared to say most branches of engineering. You don't see civil engineers coming up with cool new ways to build bridges every few years, especially not cool new ways that turn out to be more expensive and less safe than traditional techniques).

Those of us who have been around a while remember the fads. If you are not from an IT background, forgive me while I reminisce for the next page or so. Read along and see if you recognise some of the IT madness that you have observed. There is a point to it.

---

[1] Gartner is an IT industry analyst firm: www.gartner.com
[2] See Wikipedia: en.wikipedia.org/wiki/Hype_cycle

For those who were there, remember how all data was in flat files but relational databases were coming and they were going to fix everything? We followed "the one true Codd[1]". Once we had all our data in one place, referential problems and inconsistencies would vanish. With SQL all programming would be easy, and we wouldn't need many programmers anyway because users would write their own queries.

I got my start programming and teaching 4GLs[2], the end of COBOL and other crude 3GLs for ever. Once again, the end of programming was nigh as end users could learn to write such simple languages. They said the same thing about COBOL, the "business-oriented language", when my Dad learnt about it in the 1970s - but this time it was really true. Really.

Then we all built vast corporate data models. Once we got all our definitions in one place, and achieved third normal form[3] across the organisation, then all the answers would just fall out. I worked on one project that had four and a half thousand beautifully normalised tables. Boy that really helped those end users write their SQL. Slowed those 4GLs down too, and hardware hadn't gotten cheap yet – we were still running IBM 370s.

Next, CASE[4] tools were going to transform programming. Once we generated code in one place, end-users would draw pictures and finished applications would burst forth automatically. Twenty years on that one still hasn't laid down and died.

---

[1] Dr Edgar J. ("Ted") Codd, IBM researcher; "inventor" of relational database and normalization; creator of the sacred Codd's 12 Rules.
[2] 4GL: fourth generation language
[3] Third normal form or 3NF is a sacred state of data purity
[4] CASE: Computer Aided Software Engineering

Structured programming, modular programming, object-oriented programming (once we get all the methods defined in one place...), information engineering, repository (once all the meta-data is defined in one place...), RAD[1], JAD[2], directory (once all the data is indexed so it looks like it is in one place....), data warehousing (once we have a copy of all the data in one place...), EAI[3] (once we glue it all together automagically so it looks like it is in one place...), MIS[4] and then EIS[5] (once the executives have all the key data in one place....), CRM[6] (once all the customer interactions are kept in one place...), extreme programming, content management (once all the documents are in one place...), HTML, ERP[7] (once we have the whole damn business in one place...), Web Services (once all the APIs are dynamically linked, and the UDDI lets us look up everything in one place...), and of course e-commerce [embarrassed silence while we all blush].

A decade ago it was PCs, client/server and three-level architectures to decentralise everything. Now it is browsers, thin clients, blades and virtual machines to centralise everything.

Every one of them has added a little value and a lot of complexity to IT. Not one has been the silver bullet the vendors and consultants had us believe. Every one cost more and delivered less than promised. Is it any wonder the business is cynical? Not that they have a right to toss too many stones about. While all this was going on in the data-centre, over in the boardroom we had Quality Circles, BPR[8],

---

[1] RAD: Rapid Application Development
[2] JAD: Joint Application Development
[3] EAI: Enterprise Application Integration
[4] MIS: Management Information Systems
[5] EIS: Executive Information Systems, presumably more refined than mere Management Information Systems
[6] CRM: Customer Relationship Management
[7] ERP: Enterprise Resource Planning, as in SAP
[8] BPR: Business Process Re-engineering

zero based budgets, TQM[1], 6sigma, MBOs[2], KM[3], coaching, the one minute manager, centres of excellence, intellectual capital, ISO9000, outsourcing and off-shoring, triple bottom line, and of course e-commerce ...

Every now and then innovation comes along which really does change the game, disrupt, introduce a paradigm shift, create a sea change (even the language of change has fads). There were real "tectonic shifters": the computer, the compiler, the PC, mice, the hyperlink, the internet, the virus, email, project management, supply chain management. In the hindsight of future decades, Service Management will prove to be one of these.

Before we look at Service Management, another observation is important here. The early IT shifts were in technology. Later ones were in software. More recently, IT step changes have been in process and methods. As it matures, IT is following the same path as manufacturing (technology, then control systems, then process) and other disciplines. In fact as we will see, IT is adopting much that has been learnt in other sectors.

---

[1] TQM: Total Quality Management
[2] MBO: Management By Objectives. In traditional IT mangling of English, one can have "an MBO" that one is measured by.
[3] KM: Knowledge Management

Service management

As mentioned already, the Y2K spending overhang drove new attitudes to transparency and justification. This led to new techniques (or rather new adoption of established techniques) for business alignment, especially Service Management.

Post-Y2K, organisations are demanding greater maturity from their IT departments – they want to see them run like a business, and they want to see disciplines and formalisms as if it were engineering. The current thinking in response to this can broadly be labelled as Service Management, which represents a real paradigm shift (a much-abused term that is used correctly here).

This is part of a much larger philosophical shift in society that we cannot cover here: from a product-centric industrial age to a service-centric information age. See Peter Drucker[1] and Alvin Toffler[2] for the broader social implications, and John Zachman[3] for the implications for computing. This shift takes a generation or more and is in progress now (the end of the 20th Century and the start of the 21st).

The shift caused by Service Management is to base all IT planning and management on the business and the IT services it needs, i.e. delivering to the users of the services, instead of starting from underlying technology, from the stuff we have to build services with. This is a "customer centric" approach, which is very much in vogue in areas other than IT as well as being a fundamental of the rise of the Information Age.

---

[1] *The Post Capitalist Society*, P. Drucker, Harper Business 1994
[2] *The Third Wave*, A. Toffler, Morrow 1980
[3] *Enterprise Architecture: The Issue of the Century*, J. Zachman, Database Programming and Design, Miller Freeman, 1997

There is a matrix that can be drawn, of the technology silos that IT manages on one axis mapped against the services that technology delivers to the business on the perpendicular axis. Service Management is about turning the IT department around 90° so they look outwards at the services they provide to the business instead of looking in at the layers of their technology.

That is to say, service management is about getting IT people (or in fact any provider of a service) to think first about what matters to the user of the service and only then derive from that what is required of the technology and systems that provide the service. The users don't care what machinery is required to deliver the service so much as what comes out of the pipe.

The cultural shift from product to service has left behind IT in large organisations. They have been split off as a separate tribe with their own language and culture while the business has moved on and expectations have changed. Drawing on the advanced ideas of the Manufacturing sector, Service Management has grown up within IT (hence the term ITSM) in an attempt to heal the rift and bring corporate computing into the new age. We are seeing a new development now where IT is taking Service Management back to the business as an effective methodology for introducing customer-centric culture and processes across the organisation.

As a result of this shift in perspective, a second change results. Service management forces an IT organisation to think and structure itself around the services it delivers and hence the processes delivering those services, instead of around internal functional layers or technologies.

Finally, a third change results from starting with business strategy: it gets people thinking about strategy.

Once we understand what services we provide and what the users need from those services, we can plan, spend, operate, measure and improve on that basis. This is a very powerful concept that has widespread applications, and we will see much more of it in future.

Service Management applies the TQM concepts of customer-defined quality, continuous improvement, and measurement-based management. Services are defined in the terms of the people who use them. So are the levels at which the services are to be delivered. The starting points are the strategy and goals of the business, and how computing needs to support them. Services and service levels are agreed formally with the customers (ITIL distinguishes between the users who consume the service and the customers who pay for them).

Processes and roles are structured around these services, not around the technology. For example: problem, change, availability, service levels; not servers, networks, applications, desktop. Suppliers' contracts must support the service level agreements.

The technology comes last: what is required to fulfil the services now and in the forecasted future. If it doesn't make sense in terms of services and processes, we don't need it.

The focus is on maintaining and continuously improving quality of service. Service levels are measured. Processes are refined to improve them. This is an example of how ideas from the manufacturing industries have been showing up in the service industries.

Service Management has respectable antecedents, a good body of practical experience and good alignment with the macro-level trends in society. It is real. But that does not automatically mean we should all rush out and do ITIL.

I interviewed a Unix systems programmer in a bank once about the machines he "owned". I asked him what applications ran on them. He started listing HP-UX, Oracle, OpenView... No, I said, *applications*; what business processes? He looked surprised and just slightly embarrassed, because he had no idea.

Alternatives to ITIL

To look and listen around the IT industry these days one would think Service Management means ITIL, but there is actually more than one game in town.

Variants and alternatives

- The ITSM Library[1], published by itSMF. For interesting historical reasons, itSMF find themselves owning and approving an "alternate" set of books originating out of the Netherlands, mostly based around ITIL but often cheaper and often easier to follow.

- MOF[2] from Microsoft is of course focused on their own Windows environment. It is a little different to ITIL (how unusual that Microsoft should create their own, slightly incompatible, version of a standard). Talk is always that future versions will 'return to the fold'. In 2008 Microsoft released version 4.0 under a Creative Commons licence, effectively putting it into the public domain.

- USMBOK[3] is an extensive body of knowledge that has had a rocky history but also has enthusiastic supporters. We recommend the *Guide[4]* for those who want a complete reference framework for Service Management that is independent of ITIL or any other body of knowledge.

---

[1] www.itsmfbooks.com/index.php?cPath=4_421
[2] *Microsoft Operating Framework*, Microsoft Corporation, www.microsoft.com/technet/itsolutions/cits/mo/mof/default.mspx
[3] Universal Service Management Body of Knowledge™ www.usmbok.org
[4] *The Guide to the Universal Service Management Body of Knowledge*, I. Clayton, Tahuti 2008, ISBN: 978-0-9814691-0-2

- A guide[1] published by the Help Desk Institute takes, not surprisingly, a call-centre slant on ITIL.

- COBIT [2] is a very comprehensive and widely embraced "checklist" for audit, with recent focus due to Sarbanes-Oxley compliance.

The IT Skeptic believes that COBIT has matured to the point where the supporting books constitute a body of knowledge (BOK) that presents a credible alternative to ITIL.

Those who say " COBIT is the what and ITIL the how" (even COBIT itself says this) either haven't read COBIT, are oversimplifying or are being excessively polite to ITIL.

ITIL goes into more depth in places, but to say COBIT sits over the top is to grossly understate the overlap. COBIT extends a long way down into the "how". I haven't done or seen a detailed "depth of how" mapping but my guess is that COBIT is as comprehensive a description as ITIL in some areas. And it covers areas ITIL (even ITIL3) doesn't.

A white paper[3] identifying the mapping between ITIL and COBIT (produced in cooperation by both groups) identified the following 9 areas of COBIT not covered by ITIL3 *at all*

- PO2 Define Information architecture

- PO3 Determine Technological direction

- PO6 Communicate management aims and direction

- PO7 Manage IT human resources

---

[1] *Implementing Service and Support Management Processes: A Practical Guide*, Higday-Kalmanowitz and Simpson Ed., Van Haren, 2005, ISBN 1-933284-37-4
[2] *COBIT 4.0,* IT Governance Institute, 2005, ISBN 1-933284-37-4
www.isaca.org/AMTemplate.cfm?Section=Overview&Template=/ContentManagement/ContentDisplay.cfm&ContentID=22940
[3] *Mapping of ITIL v3 With COBIT 4.1*, IT Governance Institute 2008, ISBN 978-1-60420-035-5,
www.isaca.org/TemplateRedirect.cfm?template=/ContentManagement/ContentDisplay.cfm&ContentID=44582

- PO10 Manage projects

- DS7 Educate and train users

- ME2 Monitor and evaluate internal control

- ME3 Ensure compliance with external requirements

- ME4 Provide IT governance

It also identifies 17 more processes only partly addressed by ITIL3.

COBIT suffers a bit from the ITIL V1 and V2 problem of too many books: it is a fragmented BOK with multiple perspectives. This is great in terms of being able to find a view of the BOK to suit any situation, but it makes it more challenging to find the right view. Funding those consultants again.

Look at the IT Skeptic's favourite: *COBIT Control Practices*[1]. Add to it the *IT Assurance Guide*[2] for assessment, the *IT Governance Implementation Guide*[3] for measurement, and *COBIT User's Guide for Service Managers*[4].

Put them all together and you have a hefty BOK on the "how" of IT Service Management that rivals ITIL. But it's not considered polite to say so and spoil ITIL's day (or decade) in the spotlight.

Benchmarks

If you just want to assess your capability, i.e. measure/benchmark your business, then there are several

---

[1] *COBIT Control Practices: Guidance to Achieve Control Objectives for Successful IT Governance*, 2nd Edition, IT Governance Institute, ISACA 2007, ISBN 978-1933284873

[2] *IT Assurance Guide: Using COBIT*, IT Governance Institute, ISACA 2007, ISBN 978-1933284743

[3] IT *Governance Implementation Guide: Using COBIT and Val IT*, 2nd Edition, IT Governance Institute, ISACA 2007, ISBN 978-1933284750

[4] Details not available at time of publication but this book should be available by the time you read this. The author was a reviewer of this book.

alternatives that are backed by a standard or standardised metrics. There is no agreed standard for measuring ITIL: every consulting firm, including itSMF itself, use a different methodology to get different answers. ITIL is about defining "how" not "how well".

- ISO20000[1] (and its ancestor BS15000) is the closest thing to an "ITIL assessment standard". Despite some impressions given to the contrary, these are not 100% the same as ITIL. See "A standard", p20.

- COBIT (see above) or the lighter COBIT Quickstart[2]

- The "owners" of CMM, Carnegie Mellon, have produced the eSourcing Capability Model[3]. It provides incremental assessment for IT services. It includes both a service provider model and a client model. It claims to be applicable whether internally or externally sourced but is generally viewed as an outsourcing model. It also addresses the governance issues that arise in a multi-vendor environment. eSCM contains both a best practices model and an assessment methodology. Since its inception reportedly only 10 companies have certified in eSCM so whatever its merits it is hardly a runaway success.

- The IT Service Capability Maturity Model[4] also uses the CMM maturity measurement model. It has had little uptake since its release in January 2005. It seems to be the proverbial "three guys in a garage" who have taken the "build it and they will come" approach. Guys, they won't.

---

[1] ISO 20000-2:2005 IT Service Management Standard: Code of practice for service management, International Standards Organisation, 2005
[2] *COBIT Quickstart*, IT Governance Institute, 2003, ISBN 1-893209-59-8
[3] itsqc.cmu.edu/models/index.asp
[4] *The IT Service Capability Maturity Model*, Niessinka, Clerca, Tijdinka, and van Vlietb, CIBIT, 2005, www.itservicecmm.org

...and other new approaches are emerging all the time. This is still a maturing area.

Simpler frameworks

If you are looking for something simpler than ITIL, then there are several options:

- Check out "ITIL Lite", *ITIL Small-Scale Implementation*[1]. This is an official ITIL book that attempts to scale ITIL down for smaller businesses. It looks useful but note that smaller organisations are not the same thing as SME (small to medium enterprise). ITIL Small-Scale is about as light as some 'lite' snack foods: it is still a lot to digest. The 1998 version[2] seemed to be good but it got very little attention; it remains to be seen how the latest version goes or what the results will be. (By the way, what a great name the old book had: "ITIL in SITU" – small IT units - how could they not reuse that?). The latest 2008 version is an official complementary book for ITIL3.

- FITS[3] does not get anything near the attention it deserves. Developed for UK schools, it is a nice simplification of ITIL that really is workable in an IT shop of one person or a few people.

- ISM[4], the "out-of-the-box" solution for IT Service management". Always a bold claim but if anyone can pull it off Jan van Bon can.

---

[1] *ITIL Small-scale Implementation*, Office of Government Commerce, The Stationery Office Books, 2008, ISBN 9780113310784
[2] *IT Infrastructure Library practices in Small IT Units*, Office of Government Commerce, The Stationery Office 1998
[3] Online content at becta.org.uk/fits/index.cfm, or for a book read *FITS pocket guide*, Becta, Becta, 2004. publications.becta.org.uk/display.cfm?resID=25868
[4] *Integrated Service Management* www.ismportal.nl/nl/ism-out-box-solution-it-servicemanagement

- Core Practice[1] (CoPr or "copper") is an interesting new development that bears watching[2] (see p44). A conceptual framework exists but virtually no content and even less community support... so far.

Adjoining frameworks

Around the edges of ITIL there are other frameworks. Depending on what you want to achieve perhaps Service Management is not your core focus. There are "near-by" frameworks and methodologies, of which this is just a sampling:

- Software development and acquisition: CMMI-DEV[3], ASL[4], BiSL[5], CMMI-ACQ[6], ISPL[7]

- Security: ISO27001[8]

- Project management: MSP[9], M_o_R[10], PMBoK[11] and PRINCE2[12].

- Governance: ISO38500[13], IT Balanced Scorecard[14]

---

[1] www.corepractice.org/

[2] Disclosure: the author is involved in this project

[3] CMMI for Development
www.sei.cmu.edu/publications/documents/06.reports/06tr008.html

[4] Application Services Library www.aslbislfoundation.org/uk/asl/index.html

[5] Business information Services Library
www.aslbislfoundation.org/uk/bisl/index.html

[6] CMMI for Acquisition
www.sei.cmu.edu/publications/documents/07.reports/07tr017.html

[7] Information Services Procurement Library projekte.fast.de/ISPL

[8] ISO/IEC 27001:2005 Information technology -- Security techniques -- Information security management systems – Requirements
www.iso.org/iso/catalogue_detail?csnumber=42103

[9] Managing Successful Programmes www.apmgroup.co.uk/MSP/MSPHome.asp

[10] Management of Risk www.apmgroup.co.uk/M_o_R/MoR_Home.asp

[11] *A Guide to the Project Management Body of Knowledge (PMBOK® Guide)*, PMI, PMI 2004, ISBN 9781930699458

[12] PRojects IN Controlled Environments
www.apmgroup.co.uk/PRINCE2/PRINCE2Home.asp

[13] ISO/IEC 38500:2008 Corporate governance of information technology
www.iso.org/iso/catalogue_detail?csnumber=51639

[14] *The IT Balanced Scorecard Revisited*, A. Cram, Information Systems Control Journal Volume 5, 2007
www.isaca.org/Template.cfm?Section=Home&CONTENTID=35667&TEMPLATE=/ContentManagement/ContentDisplay.cfm

- Industry verticals: Basel II1 for banking, or eTOM2 for telecommunications.

- Quality: TQM3, ISO90004, Baldrige5 and SixSigma6.

Recommendations

7. Don't get swept away on a tide of ITIL. After determining what changes and improvements to culture and process you need to make, then (and only then) take a look at what best suits your business. ITIL is very good at what it does. It may be the right thing for you. Or not.

---

[1] en.wikipedia.org/wiki/Basel_II

[2] www.tmforum.org/browse.aspx?catID=1647

[3] Total Quality Management en.wikipedia.org/wiki/Total_Quality_Management

[4] ISO 9001:2000 Quality management systems -- Requirements www.iso.org/iso/iso_catalogue/management_standards/iso_9000_iso_14000/iso_9000_essentials.htm

[5] Baldrige National Quality Program baldrige.nist.gov

[6] en.wikipedia.org/wiki/Six_Sigma

The Future of ITIL

There can be no dispute that ITIL is currently top of the heap among IT Operations bodies of knowledge. Given the volatility of the IT industry it can be assumed it will not stay there for long, so the question is how long?

Certainly ITIL will stay on top long enough to be useful, and even when it is displaced from top position, its replacement is likely to be built upon ITIL foundations, so that an organisation will be able to build and grow into whatever comes after. What that might be is anyone's guess at this time (2008).

In the short term, someone could produce an equivalent library to ITIL but more precisely aligned to the ISO 20000 standard, or to COBIT. Both of these frameworks define how to measure practices but provide less practical advice than ITIL does on how to do the practices, and how to set them up. But if they did, things might rapidly change.

In fact COBIT is rapidly approaching a state where it provides a complete and credible alternative to ITIL. Probably it is too similar to ITIL, so that any advantages to switching would be outweighed by ITIL's acceptance and momentum, unless things go horribly wrong in the ITIL world. In that case Microsoft may succeed in their plans to rule the world and MOF could displace ITIL.

More likely something less predictable will grow from left field to challenge ITIL's dominion. It is safe to say[1] that this is several years off at least, making ITIL a worthwhile undertaking now, where the business case supports it.

---

[1] "It is safe to say". Famous last words for all prognosticators.

Whatever emerges, it will almost certainly gain top spot because it has a broader scope, perhaps encompassing service, governance and assurance[1]; or IT solutions and development as well as operations; or all of business operations including IT, finance, logistics, HR and so on. Hopefully ITIL will still form a subset, or be very similar.

Of course if Service Management gets totally discredited or swept away by some alternate worldview, then ITIL will be dead.

---

[1] "Assurance" is used here to cover areas like risk, audit, security and compliance

What to Watch Out For

ITIL is not perfect. The material has its quirks and flaws. But it is good enough to be useful. This book does not canvas the shortcomings of the content[1]. What we do seek to provide here is a survey of the shortcomings in the thinking around ITIL. Unless noted these are all applicable to any version of ITIL. As a decision-maker tasked with approving or overseeing an ITIL project, these are the actions or attitudes or statements to watch out for, with recommendations on how to deal with them.

---

[1] The reader is referred to *I Think Something is Missing From ITIL*, Clayton Peasley and Sutherland, Red Swan 2006, ISBN 1933703067

Best practice as a given

As business commentator Mark Di Somma says[1]:

> Focused and achieved excellence is powerful, whereas striving for excellence everywhere (and not achieving it anywhere) is much less competitive. Better to be unbreakable everywhere and unbeatable in selected places than to attempt to be unbeatable everywhere, and not get there!

Di Somma has also said "World class best practice looks like everyone else". Gaining a competitive edge or differentiating yourself is not about doing what everyone else does.

It is not ITIL that is the issue here, so much as the uncritical acceptance of best practice as the only acceptable standard for everything. Take a look at what Core Practice[2] has to say:

> Not everyone can afford or wants best practice. We fully support best practices for those organisations that have the commitment and resources and reason to adopt best practice *[within specific domains of the business]*. For those who do not, something more pragmatic is required... For these organisations (e.g. small businesses, start-ups, and the cash-strapped) there is Core Practice. "If you do nothing else, do these things."
>
> We call it CoPr, pronounced "copper". Why copper? Well, because that is how the acronym sounds, obviously. But also because it isn't gold. You want the gold version? There are plenty of organisations who will sell you the gold version. This is the copper version. It is nearly as pretty and has all the same properties (near enough), but for a lot less cost.
>
> Best Practice has become something of a sacred cow in business. It is taken as a given that organisations

---

[1] www.markdisomma.com/upheavals.asp
[2] www.corepractice.org/

want to achieve best practice in everything they do and an organisation that doesn't is somehow less worthy than those that do. This should not be the case. Pursuing Best Practice is a strategic decision, which should be taken when there is an agreed ROI (tangible or intangible) for the resource investment required to get there...

We believe the world is ready for Core Practice: the strategic decision to minimise cost in an activity of the enterprise by implementing practices sufficient to (a) meet obligations and (b) to make processes work to a standard sufficient that risk (to the organisation and to people in its care) is reduced to some acceptable level.

[By the way, it sounds like we[1] are selling something ("but for a lot less cost"). We aren't. CoPr is a free, open source, volunteer resource. It is focused on small business for now, so it may not be the "Easy ITIL" that so many corporates are seeking, sorry.]

Recommendations

8. Implement ITIL (or any "best practice") when there is a business case for it. Where there isn't, don't flog yourself and don't weaken your organisation.

9. If you want gold, then consider the possibility of different standards of excellence that allow you to get ahead of those who are following the mainstream "best".

---

[1] The author founded the Core Practice movement.

ITIL the Cult

At times, the ITIL movement has distinct overtones of a cult. Consider this:

What defines "bad" process that "needs" ITIL?

- o   Getting a low score on an ITIL maturity model.

What is that model benchmarked against?

- o   The ITIL definition.

How do you get a better score?

- o   By being more like the ITIL definition.

Who defines the model and then measures it?

- o   The consultants who stand to profit from "fixing" the processes.

Circular reasoning don't you think?

> "This may work in practice, but I doubt it will work in theory".
> [1]

What if we measured existing processes against independent assessable metrics on usefulness to the business or value returned on investment or quality, or whatever the organisation cares about? We might find the existing

---

[1] *"The Making of a French Manager,"* J. Barsoux and P. Lawrence, Harvard Business Review (July-Aug., 1991): 58-67.
cbi.gsia.cmu.edu/papers/cbi_workingpaper-1999_03.pdf

processes don't fit the ITIL model but they work. That is, we might find there is no business case for changing.

Anyone who has been accosted in the street and offered a personality reading knows the trap that is being set here. Tell someone they are broken and then offer the secret to fixing it.

A group that defines its own measure of good and bad by comparing against its own internal reference books, then declares that those books hold the key to getting from bad to good, sounds mighty like a cult.

Listen to the cult's thinking:

The first step to reforming is often ITIL awareness training, for if they wallow in ignorance they cannot be saved. Never mind what they call their processes now; they have to know to call them the one true process. "Because you are ignorant of my framework, that makes you ignorant".

The next step is executive sponsorship. First rule of missionaries: if you want to convert the populace, try to convert their ruler.

Then we have to work out how to effect cultural change, which is a nice name for overcoming resistance. In a recent survey[1] "72 percent claim the biggest barrier to ITIL adoption in their business is organizational resistance." Well, *hello*. What makes you right and them wrong? Beware the automatic assumption that resistance must be steamrolled rather than listened to.

Beware also the onset of cultish behaviour. It is especially prevalent in the born-again ITILists who have been freshly

---

[1] *North American Information Technology Infrastructure Library (ITIL) Benchmark*, Evergreen Systems, 2006,
www.evergreensys.com/campaign/itil_benchmark_2006/blog/index.html

sheep-dipped ["sheep-dipping" = the basic ITIL Foundation training]. The more mature practitioners tend to get it bashed out of them by reality. The very experienced original authors of ITIL knew this when they made "adopt and adapt" a basic principle. That principle often seems to get lost.

Recommendations

10. Try to measure your organisation against something other than the proposed solution (see "Measuring ITIL with ITIL", p63).

11. If the organisation is resisting, perhaps there is a good reason. Re-examine the premises behind the ITIL proposal.

12. Don't let anyone get righteous with you ("I have far more experience of ITIL", "I'm an ITIL Master", "You weren't on the training").

13. Don't be fastidious about compliance ("cleanliness").

14. And most of all: reject any absolutist position ("We do it the way the book says, period.")

"Doubt is not a very agreeable state but certainty is a ridiculous one".   Voltaire

Because everyone else is

In the survey quoted previously[1]

> • 72 percent claim the biggest barrier to ITIL adoption in their business is organizational resistance. At a very distant second, 34% are not sure where to start.
>
> • ITIL is quickly becoming visible at the enterprise IT level, with 36 percent of respondents working on re-engineering enterprise IT service delivery, and 29 percent planning to leverage all 10 ITIL discipline areas *[of ITIL2]*.
>
> • Most ITIL programs are living in a potentially dangerous vacuum. While 95% selected ITIL as a framework they are using to improve IT Operations, less than 20% even showed awareness of COBIT or CMMi.
>
> "While visibility with CIOs continues to rise, the alarming combination of a lack of effective planning, organizational resistance to change and the enterprise level of change required for success in ITIL is very troubling. A large number of initiatives will fail to yield any value, and insufficient planning will be the root cause for failure to establish senior management support and funding," said Don Casson, President and CEO of Evergreen.

The writers are highlighting these facts because they want to help fix the symptom, while we will examine the underlying cause. These numbers scream out that people are embarking on ITIL projects because everyone else is.

They don't have the support of the organisation, they haven't looked at alternatives or context, and about a third are launching in holus-bolus, without proper planning, hacking

---

[1] *North American Information Technology Infrastructure Library (ITIL) Benchmark,* Evergreen Systems, 2006,
www.evergreensys.com/campaign/itil_benchmark_2006/blog/index.html

away at everything. It is unlikely that a third of organisations have processes broken in all ten ITIL2 disciplines to such an extent that there is a good business case for fixing them.

People argue you need to re-work all ten or thirteen or twenty-seven ITIL disciplines because the processes are inter-connected. The bigger ITIL grows with each version, the sillier this premise gets. Indeed, one of the greatest strengths of ITIL is the way it defines the interactions and divisions of responsibility between areas instead of considering the processes in isolation. But people implement chunks of it every day. It works. Start where the pain is, do a bit, show benefit (or not) then decide what next. Trying to do it all at once all but ensures failure.

It gets worse. From itSMF USA's own research newsletter[1]:

> Compass then asked the companies how well they actually measure their ITIL process maturity. Only 4 percent of respondents felt able to say that all of their ITIL processes were fully measured for maturity and fewer than one third of respondents had maturity measures for all ITIL processes. Compass also asked people to define how well their organization is able to relate process maturity to performance improvement based on measurement. Only 9 percent of respondents felt able to say that the relationship was based on full measures, fully linking process maturity with performance. A staggering 72 percent felt unable to acknowledge any linkage at all between process maturity and performance improvement.

Something of an "own goal", that one.

In all the statistics above we hear the march of zealots, sweeping aside reason in their quest for ITIL purity.

---

[1] *itSMFUSA Research Letter*, Volume 2, Issue 4, April 2006
data.memberclicks.com/site/itsmf/Research_Newsletter_-_April_2006_Issue.pdf

Recommendations

15. Implement ITIL because there is a business case, and for no other reason. (See the discussion of ITIL business cases, p88)

16. Do ITIL in stages. Ensure each chunk is manageable. Start where the maximum pain or payback is.

Don't expect evidence

Where is the evidence for the benefits of ITIL? There isn't any. Not the kind of hard empirical evidence that would stand up in, say, clinical trials. There is more evidence for quack alternative medicines than there is for ITIL. There is certainly more solid evidence for the application of CMM[1] in solutions development (CMM[2] is a methodology analogous to ITIL in a closely related area).

Granted there is some research around the benefits of aligning IT with the business but not around quantification of ROI[3] and nothing that the IT Skeptic is aware of that is specific to ITIL.

To be clear: the fact that ITIL itself is not based on scientific research is not the issue (here), but the business decision to invest funds in its adoption should ideally be evidence based. We are not looking for evidence to support why ITIL does something a particular way. We need evidence that doing it that way returns a benefit to the business (financial or other) sufficient to make adopting ITIL worthwhile.

What is required is solid scientific research on:

- Quantified cost/benefit analyses across a statistically significant number and diversity of organisations of adoption of ITL versus other BPR methodologies, or versus a simple process review and reorganisation, or versus implementation of a service desk product.

---

[1] *The Capability Maturity Model: Guidelines for Improving the Software Process,* Paulk, Weber, Curtis, and Chrissis, SEI Series in Software Engineering, Addison-Wesley, 1995.
[2] *CMMI Overview,* Carnegie Mellon SEI, 2005
[3] ROI: Return On Investment

- Quantified cost benefit analyses of organisations that have only done ITIL without concurrent Six Sigma or CMMI or other quality improvement programs that might have accounted for the effect, or at least compensating results for their expected effect.

- Analysis of the proportion of organisations that would actually benefit through adoption of ITIL.

This is not to say that ITIL is ineffective, only that there is no rigorous evidence that it is effective. So long as everybody - especially you the decision makers - understand that the decision to implement ITIL is currently taken based on anecdote, experience and instinct, then the decision is made with eyes wide open.

If you are making decisions based on amateur evidence from analysts and vendors (as everyone adopting ITIL does), here is an interesting result to ponder[1]:

> In a survey carried out by Bruton of 400 sites, about half of the 125 organizations which were found to have adopted ITIL made no measured improvement in terms of their service performance or the rate at which they were able to close helpdesk calls. "Some helpdesks can way outperform a site that has adopted the best practices of ITIL," said Bruton. "Best practice does not mean superior performance. *[In the ITSM industry]* It is beginning to sound that ITIL is the only way to go. It isn't. It is only one way to go."

Here is another "sponsored survey"[2]:

---

[1] *ITIL Experts Warn on Compliant Software*, Datamonitor Computerwire, 26 January 2006
www.computerwire.com/industries/research/?pid=8673D122-721B-4450-8C57-30A9665D4BA2
[2] *Firms Must Take ITIL Beyond IT Operational Goals*, R. Peynot, Forrester, March 14, 2006
i.i.com.com/cnwk.1d/html/itp/Front_Range_ITIL_Beyond_Goals.pdf

> "Did you make a business case before decision? (Base: 62 European firms): No 68%".

TWO THIRDS had no business case.

> "Did you observe the expected ROI? (Base: 20 European firms). No 50% Don't know 30% Yes 20%."

If less than a third built a business case, one would guess the ones that did represent a sample biased towards those who had a good case, and yet only ONE FIFTH of them achieved the expected ROI.

The irony is ITIL's own emphasis on the importance of a business case and ROI. But the facts are that few organisations even bother to examine the business case before embarking on ITIL; even fewer measure results; and the few that do are building their business case in the absence of any solid research to justify their estimates.

The remainder of this section to page 60 reviews the evidence you will encounter, so that you may make your own judgement call on its merit.

itSMF

The itSMF make a few unsubstantiated claims in the ITIL2 version of *An Introductory Overview of ITIL*[1]:

Over 70% reduction in service downtime

ROI up by over 1000%

Savings of £100 million per annum

New product cycles reduced by 50%.

---

[1] *An Introductory Overview of ITIL*, C. Rudd, itSMF 2004

There is no reference or other substantiation for these figures whatsoever but - given the reputable source - this quote shows up.

Academic research

Before it disappeared, the Best Practice Research Unit (BPRU) was a website[1] claiming to be associated with the ITIL3 Refresh (After twenty years of ITIL, it is high time there was such a unit.)

It is a shame there is no such initiative from either OGC or itSMF (at least itSMF USA is doing something, in fact several things focused on research).

The BPRU website explicitly recognised the evidence problem:

> Much of the material published on IT management, including IT service management, has been normative or prescriptive in flavour. Few rigorous, academic studies have been undertaken to evaluate how tools, techniques, methods and management approaches have been selected, adapted, implemented and measurable benefits achieved.
>
> There is a danger that new approaches arise out of the practitioner community with little empirical validation.

"Few rigorous, academic studies" is generous. The solitary piece of academic research the IT Skeptic found carries a bold and unproven title "Evidence that use of the ITIL framework is effective"[2]. It opens by saying "Very little academic material exists on ICT Service Management Best Practice..." and concludes its own research with:

---

[1] www.tonybetts.com/about_bpru. The site has been taken down.
[2] *Evidence that use of the ITIL framework is effective*, B.C. Potgieter, J.H. Botha, C. Lew www.naccq.ac.nz/conference05/proceedings_04/potg_itil.pdf

> We found that both customer satisfaction and operational performance improve as the activities in the ITIL framework increases. Increased use of the ITIL framework is therefore likely to result in improvements to customer satisfaction and operational performance. Although the study was limited to a single research site, claims made by executive management of the research site and OCG as to the contribution the ITIL framework seems to be justified. More definitive research delineating the nature of these "relationships" is however needed, especially regarding each process in the ITIL framework.

The data base is poor: "research site was a large service unit of ICT in a provincial government in South Africa during 2002/3." One local government site is not a good sample base.

More importantly, the two things measured to support this brave conclusion were (1) customer satisfaction (the three surveys they conducted only included management in the final survey so all we can say is that non-managerial staff were happier) and (2) "objective service improvement" by measuring "the number of calls logged at the Help Desk" because "we can rather safely conclude that the number of problems logged would be a good reflection of objective service levels". That last statement leaves this research with zero credibility with anyone who understands ITIL and ITSM.

No cost/benefit analysis. Not a single valid objective metric. If you throw enough government money at anything and launch an aggressive enough PR campaign you can make the users happier. That proves nothing. To those experienced in these things, the fact that calls to the Service Desk went down rather than up over an initial nine month period would be a cause for concern not celebration.

But you can bet this paper will be quoted all over the place as evidence of the effectiveness of ITIL, so be aware.

Analysts

The IT Skeptic introduced the concept of Crap Factoids[1]. Crap Factoids are pure bull-excrement that almost sound like a fact, and will be presented so often that everyone will think it true. The worst perpetrators of Crap Factoids are analysts (closely followed by vendors and consulting firms). It is time people called analysts to task for this because we all suffer the consequences when decision makers fall for it.

My concerns with much research published are that the 'research' is

- commissioned to prove a point, like cancer research paid for by the tobacco industry but with less observers ready to scream "foul"

- created as a revenue generating exercise, therefore the results need to be attention-getting and self-serving (grow the market)

- anecdotal and opinion-based

- asked of the wrong person – those accountable instead of objective observers: "How brilliant were you..." "Did you make the right decision to..." "What ROI have you had from your spending..."

- lacking transparency (and hence impossible to reproduce): what was the methodology? what questions were actually asked? how was the sample derived? what controls were there (generally none)? what were the raw results?

---

[1] www.itskeptic.org/crap-factoids

- unscientific. There is no control group to compare to. There is no double-blind labelling to remove researcher bias. The raw data is not disclosed to allow checking of the conclusions drawn. There is no random sampling: respondents self-select by agreeing to respond or worse still the vendors choose.

- without peer review. Where are the academic and professional journals and conferences with real review boards? (Note: the itSMF International will publish a peer-reviewed academic journal on ITSM in 2009). ? Even a peer-reviewed website for authorative vetted articles would be welcome.

Gartner are perhaps the best known of the IT industry analysts. You will see them quoted as expecting "up to a 48 percent cost reduction by applying ITSM principles". The IT Skeptic has been unable to find the original citation, in order to examine the data and methods that arrived at this figure, but it turns up regularly. It can be recognised by the authorative-sounding figure: "48%". Not 50, just 48.

There may appear to have been actual research by the analysts but close examination often reveals it is hearsay. To take just one example (from Forrester) *Application Mapping For The CMDB*[1] is nineteen pages of the benefits of application-to-infrastructure-mapping-tools ("better understanding of how applications are deployed in production ... better control of infrastructure and application changes ... possibility of controlling spiraling [sic] application costs ... better way to consolidate infrastructure ... better planning of backup sites" ... heal warts ... reconcile East and West ....) and comparison of eight tools, and not

---

[1] *The Forrester Wave: Application Mapping For The CMDB Q1 2006,* Forrester, www.cnetdirectintl.com/direct/bmc/Q3_2006/ebook/Service_Management/UK/registration.htm

one word about whether the tools are actually useful or whether application mapping works or what the limitations of the concept are.

Forrester's research into the effectiveness of the tools consisted of "customer success", which appears to have been measured solely via the vendor's own references.

For the part of the actual research that looked at functionality "Forrester looked at the product architecture for its real-time capabilities in building maps and detecting changes. We considered key issues such as time to collect data, the need for manual intervention, the depth of data collected, and the security and maintenance of the resulting CMDB." There was apparently no consideration of the usefulness of the data for managing a business service.

They did this by (a) asking the vendors and (b) asking "three companies that had conducted independent evaluations of the vendors' products". There is no information on whether these three companies had actually installed the products and to what level they tested the practicality of the results, or whether they in turn had conducted paper-based evaluations of vendor references and brochures. There is no evidence that Forrester actually saw any of these products in action, let alone installed and tested them themselves.

For the uncritical reader - and most IT people are far too busy to be critical readers - a 19-page analyst white paper with graphs and lists and tables looks authorative. Most will thumb through to the chart that shows where the products ranked, and accept the premise that this must be a good idea else people would not be selling tools or analyses to help select those tools.

More examples[1] could be found from every analyst firm in the industry so please do not get the impression that this issue is limited to the firms cited here. (For the worst abuse of fact and statistics by reputable organisations ever seen by the author, see www.itskeptic.org/node/709.)

Analysts employ clever people who often have great insights into where things are heading. They get around, crossing industry boundaries and talking to many. Their opinions are interesting. They almost always explain things more clearly than the vendors can. So their product is worth reading... but not, in general, for the research.

Always bear in mind that analysts exist to create change so that they may interpret it. They will always promote the next big thing because the uncertainty it induces is their lifeblood. Analysts should call themselves what they are: marketing outsourcers. At least the vendors are overt about it. So take analyst statistics with a very large pinch of salt.

Recommendations

17. Don't expect an evidence-based business case. Have a methodology (determine your organisation's practice) for evaluating subjective business cases.

18. Look sceptically at evidence proffered. Reject any that is analyst/vendor hearsay and guesstimate. Evaluate the remaining business case on its merits.

---

[1] See www.itskeptic.org/analysts.

You don't 'do' ITIL

Watch for proposals that talk about "implementing ITIL" or "putting in place Incident Management" or "doing Change Management". This may point to limited understanding of ITIL (though everyone expresses it that way at times). You don't implement a process, you improve it. (See also our comments later in this book regarding how the project is better described as a transformation than an implementation).

Everyone already does some form of Incident Management. The question is how well they do it. This is usually measured by a CMM maturity level, from 1 to 5. If someone says they have no process, they do really[1]: they are at level 1. Things still happen. People try to restore service. They just do it in an anarchic fashion.

ITIL is about Continual Service Improvement, and it does it by providing model processes to use as a target or ideal in defining and documenting and measuring and managing and improving our own processes.

So you don't implement Incident Management: you try to lift your maturity in Incident Management, from say 1 to 3.

This improvement is a continuous process. The initial project to enhance processes is only the first step. There must be an ongoing quality improvement program to protect, consolidate, and build on any gains made; else the organisation will slip back again.

---

[1] Almost always. I once met a site which had no detectable Problem Management process, and another site where there was zero change or release management: code existed in production and developers changed the production code as they saw fit... on an IBM System370 mainframe.

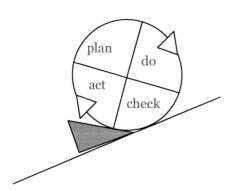

If you are familiar with the Deming Cycle, look for its application. If there is no provision for ongoing maintenance of the processes in the proposal - if they are not "chocking the wheel" of the Deming Cycle to prevent it rolling backwards again - then this is another indicator of inadequate understanding of the fundamentals.

Recommendations

19. Expect ITIL proposals to have target maturity levels for proposed processes (and an assessment of current maturity levels).

20. Ensure the proposal includes provision for ongoing measurement, maintenance and improvement of processes. Your organisation will have its own policy on whether this needs to be part of any cost estimates or ROI calculations.

21. Use resulting maturity level as a key KPI for the project. But watch out for that cultish measuring-ITIL-with-ITIL: have another independent measure too (see Measuring ITIL with ITIL, p63).

Measuring ITIL with ITIL

It is difficult to find good metrics for measuring the effectiveness of ITIL.

The usual solution is to measure ITIL in terms of raising maturity. As discussed in "ITIL the Cult", p46, this can be a circular argument: doing ITIL will make you better at doing ITIL.

Success is defined in terms of measuring maturity as benchmarked against the ITIL processes, so therefore by definition implementing ITIL will increase ITIL maturity. That doesn't mean the money was well spent, and it doesn't measure whether it was or not.

Some ITIL proponents protest that the absence of ITIL means one cannot benchmark the starting state because one is not collecting the "right" data. This is a fallacy created by trying to measure ITIL with ITIL.

Recommendations

22. Consider using COBIT (or eSCM or ISO20000) to measure your organisation's maturity. It provides accessible, structured metrics that do an excellent job of IT audit and benchmarking.

23. You will probably need to commission assessment by consultants, but before you do, download COBIT[1] (unlike ITIL it is free and in the public domain), and evaluate whether you could "roll your own" assessment.

24. Set KPIs that reflect the real business motivations for the ITIL project. If the business case for the project was to

---

[1] www.isaca.org

improve availability then measure the project on availability. If it was to improve customer service then survey satisfaction before and after.

25. Consider direct measurement of cultural maturity. The ultimate objective is to change the way people behave, so measure ABC: Attitudes, Behaviour and Culture. Bring in experts in this area to conduct assessments before and after. You need HR consultants not IT consultants.

A client said to me "But if we measure customer satisfaction as the KPI instead of ITIL process compliance, they may cheat and find other ways to improve ratings other than by using ITIL". To which I replied "So?"

If IT ain't broke don't fix it

Perhaps the saddest sight in the ITIL world is organisations that adopt ITIL processes when the old ones were working OK.

The IT Skeptic has renovated three houses now. In all cases they were fit for habitation already. It was not money well spent: the house didn't leak, the doors were secure, it was sanitary and there was no fire risk. So renovation was just for our own satisfaction. It was overcapitalising - we would not get a good ROI when we sold the house.

If I want to spend my money changing the way my house looks it is my right: it is my money. ITIL project money isn't mine. So often, adopting ITIL is like ripping up perfectly good carpet so you can polish the floorboards: it is very satisfying but there is no business case for it.

IT operations are a domain that tends to attract perfectionists. This is a good thing when sites are aiming for three-, four- or five-nines [99.999% availability]. The unfortunate aspect of perfectionists is that they can't leave well enough alone – they suffer from Excessive Technical Fastidiousness (ETF)[1]. Many technical people like completeness and accuracy, and neat, clever, intricate solutions whether there is a problem or not. The result is ETF: an obsession with doing it right, whether or not this is a useful use of time, yields a good return on investment, or is the most sensible use of available funds – i.e. whether or not it makes business sense.

---

[1] ETF is a concept introduced in the IT Skeptic's first book, *Introduction to Real ITSM*, R. England, Custom Books 2008, ISBN 1438243065, see also www.realitsm.com

Others make changes because change is power. That great business commentator of the late 20th century, Scott Adams said[1]: "change is good for the people who are causing the change. They understand the new information that is being added to the universe. They grow smarter in comparison to the rest of us".

Then we have that phenomenon The New CIO (or Operations Manager). You know the one: brought in to make some changes. Or because they are new they feel the need to make some changes. The good managers find what works and leave it alone.

For all these reasons, projects, including ITIL projects, spring up because somebody thinks it is a good idea. The increasing rigour and accountability of IT financial management means this happens less often than in the past, but it still happens.

Recommendations

26. Look beyond the "because I think so" or "because everybody else is" arguments.

27. Look beyond solid evidence that it will be better. So what? Why does it need (in business terms) to be better? Does the status quo fail to meet current and forecast business requirements?

28. If it works, leave it alone. Spend the money where it is most effective.

---

[1] *The Dilbert Principle: A Cubicle's-Eye View of Bosses, Meetings, Management Fads & Other Workplace Afflictions,* S. Adams, Collins, 1997 ISBN-13: 978-0887308581

I worked for a software vendor, a big one. I was present when our CIO was interviewed by a journalist for the IT press, who asked if we used ITIL ourselves in-house. Now you need to know this is a big shop: mainframes, huge storage farm, worldwide network, tens of thousands of users. And they sell a service desk product.

My breathing stopped as I waited to hear his answer because I knew we didn't use ITIL, and I had often whined about the fact (to colleagues who like me didn't matter): how could we sell an ITIL tool and services when we didn't even use ITIL ourselves? (though we used the tool and very well).

He replied no we didn't, because our processes were very good and delivered effective service to the business (all true). When they needed fixing he would look at the business case for ITIL.

That company cops a lot of flak but they run a tight business: the political pressure on him to be a showcase ITIL shop must have been immense, but his job was to run IT on a budget and he wasn't going to blow it on the fad du jour. I told that story with pride when challenged.

CMDB can not be done

A CMDB is a central database of information about all objects managed by ITIL, and their inter-relationships. ITIL adopted the concept of CMDB from the start. It is the only technology mandated in an otherwise process framework. ITIL2 was vague about whether CMDB had to be a single physical instance of all the data. ITIL3 is clear that it isn't, except in the places where it is vague.

Look carefully at any project proposal to see to what extent a Configuration Management Database (CMDB) is planned. The IT Skeptic maintains that CMDB can not be done as ITIL defines it with a justifiable return on the investment of doing it - it is such an enormous undertaking that any organisation attempting it is going to burn money on an irresponsible scale. Organisations that need to get their Configuration Management processes to a CMM maturity of 4 or 5 are probably going to have to attempt it; others will generally struggle to cost-justify the effort.

Put another way: a corporate jet might even show a ROI if well utilised. Whether that would be the optimum use of competing funds is another matter.

It should be disclosed that this is a minority opinion, but not a lonely one. The CMDB engenders much debate[1]. You can finds more on CMDB on the *Owning ITIL* website[2]. In brief, the requirements are complex, especially the amount of data to be gathered and maintained, the integration of systems, and the compliance and audit requirements.

---

[1] www.itskeptic.org/cmdb
[2] www.itskeptic.org/owningitil

CMDB as ERP for IT

It has been argued that CMDB integrates data for IT in the same way that ERP systems do for the enterprise as a whole.

Whether ERP is a justifiable project is in itself a fascinating debate - we've all seen ERP bring companies to the brink of ruin ... or over it. I never saw an ERP project run to business case projections.

There are organisations big enough, diverse enough and screwed enough that ERP might just return on the investment.

But to say it justifies CMDB is like saying that because DHL use jumbo jets to ship freight, DHL should also use them to get the milk for the cafeteria. Just because a mega-gazillion software behemoth provides the ERP of a total organisation does not mean that something like it is a sensible use of funds just to manage the objects in the IT environment.

What happens is that ITIL convinces IT people they need a jumbo but they only have budget for a billy-cart. Then they get up on the roof and the inevitable happens.

Living without CMDB

Neither ERP, relational database, data-dictionary, repository, nor directory succeeded in unifying our environments. Nor will CMDB (nor Web Services nor SOA nor .NET nor ...). Lighten up and stop trying to find one repository to rule them all. Let our data be a little untidy. Let go of that old "everything has to be complete and correct" mindset. Live without CMDB.

People are doing fine without CMDB now. In statistics for implementation of ITIL processes, Configuration Management is always one of the lowest percentages. One

2008 survey[1] said 30% of very large organisations (those who can afford it) claimed to have something they called a CMDB. The IT Skeptic estimates[2] that between 2% and 5% of IT organisations have a fully-implemented as-defined-by-ITIL CMDB. This raises the question of what everyone else does without a CMDB.

Incident-Problem-Change works fine on top of a single asset database. It is not that important whether Availability or Release or Continuity or Financial or other disciplines use the same repository – the perfectionists love it if they do but there is no great downside if they do not.

It is nice to store those basic "depends on" links to show the key CIs[3] which services depend on. My experience is that most organisations can manually maintain these service mappings for about ten to fifty services. Yet most have two to ten times that many services. They all seem to end up pragmatically picking the top services to store the mappings in the database. What happens to the rest? They wing it; they work it out on the fly; like they always did. It works.

You can do without CMDB, so long as you are aiming at not too high a maturity level, say 3. If we aspire to a moderate level of maturity, then yes we can do without a CMDB. Plenty of people do. They may have an asset register, a systems management tool auto-discovering the network, a purchasing system, maybe even a service catalogue. But they don't have a CMDB as defined by ITIL.

On the other hand, if you are NASA or Boeing or Tata or EDS, ignore me. You want level 5 maturity and for most processes you'll need a CMDB to get there ... or rather you'll

---

[1] *How to Develop Your CMDB Project's ROI*, EMA, 2008, whitepapers.techrepublic.com.com/abstract.aspx?docid=386941
[2] www.itskeptic.org/node/732
[3] CI = Configuration Item, ITIL geek-speak for "thing"

need to start working on a CMDB. The IT Skeptic is still not convinced you will ever get to the idealised model. It is going to cost you trying.

For more on how to deal with CMDB, see "Restrain Configuration Management", p125.

Recommendations

29. Ensure that a pragmatic approach is planned to Configuration Management, where the minimum data necessary is gathered.

30. CMDB is seldom the best place to start with ITIL. Ensure more important priorities are addressed first.

31. Develop a Service Catalogue early (see p123): do a technical version as a point of focus for IT people. In that technical Catalogue, document the key CIs that support each service. If you really want to let the geeks out for a run, record the Services in your Service Desk tool and link the key CIs there. But keep a very tight rein on this initiative; it must be *maintainable for reasonable ongoing cost*. That may be as close to CMDB as you will ever get.

At an ITIL conference once, a government IT person was telling me how his CMDB was going to be successful because he focused on what mattered and left out all sorts of irrelevant stuff. Like what, I asked?

Like desktop PCs.

So there is no application code on the PCs?. Of course it turns out the key application was client/server. OK so now PCs are in the pot.

But we won't track peripherals like printers.

Oh really, and what proportion of your helpdesk calls are for printers?

OK printers are in but not keyboards or mice.

Hmmm... but you are a government department: I bet you have to be sensitive about OSH [occupational safety and health] requirements [not to mention political correctness]. Got any disabled staff with requirements for special peripherals?

By this time he's pale and sweaty and hurrying off...

Vendor references

Few managers need to be told how suspect vendor references are, but for the sake of completeness, let us review why they should be discounted in any business case evaluation. References can be obtained by four main mechanisms:

- Love them. This requires far more vendor resource than could ever be sustained except in two or three over-serviced clients.

- Appeal to ego. Make them look a hero. Put their face on full page ads in magazines where their peers will see. Give them a poster-size framed version of the ad for their office wall.

- Bribe them. It would be interesting to see research on the number of reference sites whose CIO went to the world conference at the vendor's expense as a speaker or regularly appears on speaking tours to warm sunny countries. This works particularly well with a CIO about two years from retirement: apply #1 and #2 above so they look like a hero, then once they retire employ them on contract to be an overseas superstar keynote speaker at conferences in exotic places.

- In the face of defeat, declare victory. This was an old British military tactic when faced with unshakeable guerrilla insurgence: walk away and hold a victory parade. What CIO will admit the half-million-dollar project is a failure when they can bluff their way out of it? Tell everyone how successful it was for long enough and even your own staff might start to believe it, especially if they start getting invited to conferences in exotic places.

Recommendations

32. Discount vendor references or statistics derived from references when evaluating proposals.

33. Look to other sources, especially forums and discussion boards. These tend to attract the bitter and dissatisfied customers. As such they are equally as biased as the vendor's references. A balance of both sources might get you somewhere near an objective view.

Compliance with other methodologies

If your organisation uses RUP, SDLC, AGILE, CMM, PMI, COBIT, 6Sigma, TQM or other methodologies already, ensure any ITIL project includes an allowance for working with other stakeholders to rationalise and integrate ITIL with these, as the ITIL framework does not define any interfaces and in some instances is at variance with them.

Even ITIL3 is still not fully aligned with ISO20000, loosely known as "the ITIL standard", let alone any of these other bodies of knowledge. (See "A standard", p20)

Recommendations

34. Require consideration of other incumbent methodologies as part of the impact analysis in the business case

35. Require estimation of the work to resolve the interfaces

The benefits of ITIL

As we have seen ("Don't expect evidence", p 52), there is no concrete evidence that using ITIL to make process improvements has any benefit over any other approach to improving practices in IT operations.

You could re-engineer your processes using astrology instead of ITIL and you would see a positive result. Any process benefits from some attention. The difference between ITIL and placebo has never been researched.

In most cases ITIL is the sensible choice because of its status as de facto standard. But don't take it for granted.

Recommendations

36. Ensure alternatives (see "Alternatives to ITIL", p34) have been considered: MOF for married-to-Microsoft shops; COBIT if it fits requirements better; ISO20000 or SM-CMM for a service provider; something simpler like FITS.

37. Consider something much simpler: like any transformation of process, ITIL requires a cultural change program to bring the people along. What if the project consisted of nothing but the cultural change program? What if you gave people training in current process, showered them with some attention, ran workshops so they could be heard, and re-organised the roles and structure to better fit current process?

Questionable business cases

Forgive me if this is stating the obvious, but there is a nasty little trick that shows up in business cases (I might even have used it myself in a past life), nothing specific to ITIL business cases but used in them all too often. It goes something like this:

"Computer downtime last year resulted in $185 million in losses in the business. Downtime was 83 hours so downtime costs $37k per minute. Mean time to repair for priority 1 incidents is 150 minutes. Based on figures from a conference presentation, implementing ITIL is expected to make a 10% improvement in MTTR. Last year we had 22 priority 1 incidents, so forecast savings to the business of implementing ITIL are 22 x 150 x 0.1 x $37k = $12M p.a. for an outlay of only $7M, yielding a payback period of 7 months."

My personal favourite variation that makes the fallacy even more obvious is this one:

"blah blah blah so users will spend an average 7 minutes per day less in dealing with the Service Desk. Given 23,000 users at an average total cost per user per annum of $72k, this gives a return of $24M per annum in increased productivity".

Balls. Freeing up 7 minutes per day will allow most users one more cup of coffee, a longer linger at a colleague's cube, or an extended lunch, as if they could even detect the difference. Likewise the attempt to assign a cost per hour of downtime, or even sillier a cost per minute. Such numbers serve well to focus the minds of those responding to an incident, but that does not translate into real returns to the business for every minute saved.

Research on ITIL ROI would be a useful thing for the general information of the industry, but if you are considering whether or not to adopt ITIL, any ROI information you can find now is useless.

Your ROI will be entirely dependent on how broken your organisation is. So the fact that organisation X got $7.43 in ROI by implementing ITIL incident management is of zero interest to your organisation, unless they happen to be remarkably similar organisations.

ITIL isn't some new and magical thing that doesn't already exist in your organisation. ITIL is a transformation of existing processes from one maturity to another (hopefully higher) maturity. So the return depends totally on the current maturity levels of your organisation - how much room for improvement there is.

The average weight-loss on a particular diet is not a predictor for what I would lose, especially if I were already underweight (which I most certain am not but work with me here - it is just an analogy).

If there were tables available of average ROI in moving between any two maturity levels, and if you went to the expense of taking a read on your current ITIL maturity levels, THEN that generic ROI information would be useful in predicting your return.

But the only data available currently is the anecdotal stories that come out of the analysts and vendors about how one organisation saved a million bucks. This is (a) not a predictor of your own results and (b) usually bull excrement anyway.

Recommendations

38. Look for tangible returns on investment that can be banked, not funny money cooked up through questionable assumptions or anecdotal evidence.

ASP or ISP

A subtle distinction that often trips organisations up is in what kind of services are provided to the business or the business wants to be provided with.

Remember ASPs (Application Service Providers)? Now more commonly called on-demand or Software as a Service (SaaS). In the late 90s ASPs were going to change the face of business. They didn't, though some interesting examples are doing well, such as SalesForce.com and ... oh ... um ... SalesForce.com.

Actually a few other examples are coming along, including several ITIL-related ones, the best known of which is service-now.com, an on-demand service desk system.

Many IT departments are effectively an ASP within the business[1]. They are serving up applications, providing all the hosting and maintenance, and at least hoping to charge for it on some per-use basis. In this case, the business does not care about the underlying infrastructure. IT is a black-box. The users don't want to know about the pumps, just what comes out of the pipe: payroll, warehousing, ordering, accounts...

However in a significant number of cases, what business units want is an Infrastructure Service Provider, or ISP (and you thought the "I" meant "Internet"). The business wants to take some responsibility for their applications, and looks to IT for platform (servers, operating systems, desktops, databases, network...), storage, bandwidth, and operations (security, availability, backup and recovery...). This is

---

[1] I guess that makes them a snake in the grass. Seriously though, the buzzword used to be Internal Corporate Service provider or ICSP but that seems to have fallen by the wayside too.

common in geeky departments like engineering but can crop up anywhere.

Neither ASP nor ISP is "correct". Whether one or the other model is preferred (or prohibited) should be defined in the IT part of the business strategic plan, but that is outside the scope of this book.

What is important is for all parties to be clear on what the model is. I have seen confusion and disagreement vanish the moment people realised they were talking on different levels.

Note: this distinction between ASP and ISP just might be covered in the new ITIL3 core book *Service Strategy* but who would know? (For those who have not yet had the pleasure of reading it, this author said of *Service Strategy* in a review[1] "It will take a year of exploration to absorb it, another year to really understand it especially in a practical context, and more time still to prioritise the insights. The whole ITSM community will be chewing on *Service Strategy* for years to come. Quite a few will find it indigestible. Others will find it full of long-term nourishment.")

Recommendations

39. In all discussions of what the IT services are or could be, start with a definition of ASP and ISP, and then check everyone is on the same wavelength in any issue.

40. In the Service Catalogue, be clear what model each service belongs to.

41. In any argument about services, check that the cause is not a mismatch of mental models between ISP and ASP.

---

[1] *ITIL Version 3 Service Strategy: An Early Review*, The IT Skeptic, www.itskeptic.org/owningitil

What to Ask From ITIL

We have looked at some of the traps and dangers to watch for in an ITIL project.   More positively now, let us consider what ITIL can deliver and how you measure it.

The artefacts produced by an ITIL project are documents, tools, communications, events and sometimes organisational structures and roles.

These products are created in order to describe and manage new ways of doing the processes to get the IT operations job done. So a more important visible output of an ITIL project should be new processes in action.

But the primary objective of any ITIL project must be cultural change: change the mindset, attitudes and behaviour of the IT operations staff (and to a lesser extent their users). Culture, in a business context, is just a fancy name for "how we approach things round here".

If there is no – or insufficient - cultural change, there can be no long-term project success.

In some projects, the processes never see the light of day. There is a small mountain of documentation produced after a flurry of assessment, benchmarking, consultation, work-shopping and design – activities that the consultants feast upon. Training is delivered, forms are posted, expensive new software installed, manuals printed and distributed, new portals appear on the intranet. Then life goes on as before. The tool is never adopted beyond some pilot group, the processes are ignored or circumvented, and the manuals gather dust.

Other projects count themselves as a success because the process goes into operation. But after a year or two the actual process has drifted away from the documented one, many controls have been relaxed or subverted, uptake has not expanded to all forecast departments or processes, subsequent phases have been forgotten, the project has been disbanded and ownership lost, and the organisation is slipping back to where it was before the project. It didn't stick.

Failure to implement anything, or failure to maintain momentum, is almost invariably due to neglecting People, the first of our three key factors: People Process and Technology (and yet it is the last of the three – technology - that is often blamed).

We often talk about "implementing" ITIL or "doing" ITIL. These are the wrong words but we all use them, including this author. ITIL is a **transformation** not an implementation. The processes are there already - we just change them to a standardised (supposedly best) way of doing them. We transform them through process re-engineering, and we keep them that way through cultural change.

If the process works, technology can make it more efficient and better measured and managed. If the process doesn't work or the people don't accept it, the technology just wastes your money. "People Process Technology, in that order" – make it a mantra.

I was commissioned to prepare Service Desk/Incident/Problem/Change processes to support a client's new core IT system. Interviewing a wide range of staff, I found many ad-hoc processes stumbling along. It was the typical anarchic site; people knew their own piece of the process, nobody had the whole picture, nothing was documented, nothing much had been planned. It just grew.

One day I'm interviewing one of the applications support team at his desk. I spy a chart pasted to the wall behind him and become distracted: it looks like a flowchart of a very detailed incident management process. I look closely: it is! I ask if I can have it. "Oh yeah, help yourself. No-one follows that."

It was a bit like an engineer hacking his way through the jungle to survey a road and coming across ruins of asphalt and concrete with a median barrier down the middle.

Cultural Change

More than any other outcome, the thing we most hope for from an ITIL project is a change in the mindset of the IT staff, and even the users of IT.

We look for a change in the focus of activities, especially in times of crisis. Look for thinking and behaviours and language that show:

- restoration of service is the first priority.

- tasks are prioritised based on the affected service.

- ideas are vetted based on whether they improve a service or not.

- change is controlled in order to make life easier (as compared to doing it as an administrative chore).

- users are seen as colleagues in need of help, rather than nuisances; as needing information, rather than stupid; as people to be proactively sought out to assist, rather than avoided. [1]

Recommendations

42. Measure cultural change as the primary deliverable of an ITIL transformation.

43. Listen to the "vibe" to do your own informal monitoring of culture change: what words are people using? Are they referring back to services?

---

[1] To understand how hard this shift is for some technical people, think Bruce the Shark in the movie *Finding Nemo*: "fish are friends".

Return on investment

There is no value in ITIL; there is only value in service improvement.

Service is improved in two ways; efficiency (cost reduction) or effectiveness (improved quality).

Value is recognised only if the business *wants* increased efficiency (which they might not if it involves a degradation of quality) or increased effectiveness (which they might not if involves increased costs).

So value is meaningful only in terms of what the business requires.

According to a 2004 survey[1]

> "Average cost of ITIL implementation is around £5338 per IT seat regardless of how much of IT takes part."

The breakdown of this **external** cost was about half on consultants, a third on tools and a sixth on training.

In the same survey less than a fifth of respondents saw any reduction in headcount and over half reported no change (and the rest saw an increase).

So the purpose of doing ITIL is not usually to increase efficiency.

In fact, most numbers in ITIL business cases are of the rubbery kind that will never actually be realised as released funds in a budget to be re-allocated elsewhere (see "Questionable business cases", p77), with the exception of headcount reductions.

---

[1] *The ITIL Experience: Has it been worth it?,* N. Bruton, 2004

So return on investment must be measured in intangible value (Value on Investment or VOI): reduced outages in the business, less failed changes, better customer satisfaction, faster time to support new services.

Other outcomes are even harder to quantify, and your organisation may or may not have a methodology for assigning value to such things as reduced risk or improved compliance.

Recommendations

44. Benchmark proposed external spending against the rules of thumb of:

    • half on consultants, a third on tools and a sixth on training

    • say £6,000 or US$10,000 per IT seat in 2008 terms

45. Also look at the ratio of total spending on People, Process and Technology (see p109).

46. Find a methodology to evaluate VOI, or make the decision on faith.

47. Far too much ITIL is done because IT wants to do things "better". Ask yourself:

    • Is there a VOI or ROI?

    • If there is, great but does the business *need* "better"?

    • And even if they do, is the investment the *best* use of scarce funds? (See "Don't do it", p98)

Artefacts

In terms of what an ITIL project should actually produce, the most visible thing will be quantities of documents. In addition there will usually be some new tools implemented, and sometimes some changes to the way the organisation is structured. Look for the following key documentation (along with much other content justifying the expensive consultants involved):

- A business case, including a definition of metric(s) of success: how do we know we got there

- An idealised set of processes: the "end game" that specifies target maturity levels

- Phased intermediate process design(s): step(s) of increasing maturity towards the end state

- Role-based guides[1] and training, so people can understand their part to play and not get swamped unnecessarily by the total picture

- An implementation plan, with cultural change program

- A Service Catalogue

Service Catalogue

The ITIL2 books don't make much of Service Catalogue but it is the central, pivotal, fairly-static object in the ITIL world. (The central dynamic, transactional object is the Service Desk ticketing system, and the asset database). ITIL3 makes more of Service Catalogue, but still does not place it as centrally as the IT Skeptic and others would.

---

[1] "Guides" is a much better word than "manuals". "Guides" implies brevity and relevance to a task.

Service Catalogue drives your people. It is a key mechanism in cultural change, the foundation of customer relationship, and a pivotal tool for organising effort.

Service Catalogue informs your processes. It is only once the services are defined that all the ITIL processes know what is required of them, and how to prioritise.

In the IT Skeptic's model, there are four levels of catalogue, which represent levels of maturity. Because ITIL2 and ITIL3 use "catalogue" slightly differently I thought about using another name, but "catalogue" exactly describes what people expect to find in such a document.

- **Current Catalogue**: an "as-is" snapshot that defines the current set of services being delivered. This includes legacy services which we have no intention of offering to any more users. It forms an essential artefact to focus staff on the service-oriented mindset - a touchstone - and it defines the "as-is" state. Target audience: IT.

- **Brochure Catalogue**: a high-level document written in business terms that defines what is on offer to the business. It is used by Relationship Managers to provide a basis for discussions. It is used by staff as a point of reference. In ITIL3 terminology, this is the Service Pipeline, plus those parts of the Current Catalogue that we want to continue to offer[1]. It provides a definition of the "to-be" objective. Target audience: Customers, Users.

- **Technical Catalogue**: a union of Current and Brochure catalogues to describe all services actual and potential, with extensive supplementary information. It

---

[1] The geeks amongst you can find a diagram relating this catalogue structure to ITIL's Service Portfolio Management on the Owning ITIL website at www.itskeptic.org/owningitil

is used in the ITIL processes. The SLAs - once you have them - form a part of it, and there is much else: critical components, related services, escalation paths, available training etc. Target audience: IT.

- **Automated Catalogue**: an interactive tool that allows users to browse and order services. In the most advanced manifestation, services are provisioned in response to user ordering. This idea is all the rage in late 2008, although the technology has been available for a decade – think ASP.[1] As with all of these things the technology is the easy part. The business model, the means and terms of chargeback, and most of all organisational acceptance and uptake are the real issues. And the automated tool still needs to be backed up with the three documents above. These levels complement each other, not replace each other. Target audience: Users.

The early outcome to look for is the Current Catalogue. The Brochure Catalogue and the Technical Catalogue grow over time. Many organisations will never reach the level of Automated Catalogue.

Recommendations

48. Make sure an early product of any ITIL project is a Current Service Catalogue. Look for it and set it as an early milestone to produce one (see "Do a Service Catalogue early", p123).

---

[1] Application Service Provider, now more commonly called on-demand services or SaaS, Software as a Service.

Metrics

The most important thing we want to measure to determine success of an ITIL project is cultural change. It is difficult to measure.

The two most useful approaches are customer feedback and/or a "cultural audit". Feedback is well understood and documented, cultural audits less so. There are (non-IT) consulting organisations that will measure your organisational thinking across multiple dimensions to come up with a cultural audit benchmark.

This is unrelated to an ITIL assessment (which is a Good Thing), and should not be performed by ITIL consultants: as we discussed on p46, measuring the success of ITIL in terms of ITIL is circular and cultish. So we do a baseline read of culture before the project and compare it with a new audit some period afterwards.

Next most important is to measure the effectiveness of the transformed processes. There is considerable information available about this, including some good semi-official ITIL books[1]. But always remember that measuring process performance or compliance is not exactly the same as assessing cultural change.

ITIL3's *Continual Service Improvement* book talks about Balanced Scorecard which is a classic way to get a healthy broad perspective on the effectives of the systems.

Measurement is tricky. As physics teaches us: observation always distorts the observed. In this context, measuring

[1] *Implementing Metrics for IT Service Management* , D. Smith, Van Haren, 2008, ISBN 978-9087531140
Metrics for IT Service Management, P. Brooks, Van Haren, 2006 ISBN 978-9077212691

people always distorts their behaviour towards meeting the metric target, which is never exactly the same as the desired behavioural modification. This issue is outside the scope of this book.

Recommendations

49. Measure cultural change outside of the ITIL framework.

50. Also measure the success of ITIL in terms of process improvement and compliance.

51. Finally, if you must, you can also measure ITIL against ITIL, i.e. measure the change in ITIL maturity. (See "ITIL the Cult", p46)

How to Succeed With ITIL

Now that I have cast a FOG[1] over your ITIL project, we discuss what to do about it.

In addition to the tactical recommendations already given in this book to deal with the traps and dangers, this section looks at the strategic considerations recommended for anyone managing or overseeing an ITIL project.

---

[1] Fear of God, as in "we put the FOG into them"

ITIL is a **transformation** not an implementation.

ITIL2 says little about HOW we effect this transformation. There is basic material in the ITIL2 core book *Planning to Implement Service Management[1]*. This can be summed up as two classic consultant's mechanisms: (1) "the As-Is, the To-Be and how do we get there?" and (2) Plan-Do-Check-Act.

ITIL2 makes much of Plan-Do-Check-Act (a.k.a. the Deming Cycle) in introductions and overviews, but the actual content offers very little in terms of how to operate that cycle or how to tie the proffered advice into it.

ITIL3 is curiously silent too. We hope this means a complementary publication will be forthcoming. For now four of the ITIL3 core books only make passing references with no systematic attempt to address the issue. They leave it to the *Continual Service Improvement* book to describe an improvement model that is unlike and not aligned with any other in the industry.

Since the process of implementing ITIL processes is itself a lifecycle, it could be said to be a meta-lifecycle: a lifecycle for the ITIL service lifecycle (stay with me here). That is to say, because the books describe how to carry a Service through the lifecycle, along the way they almost accidentally provide a fair amount of guidance on how to implement the infrastructure for doing that carrying. There is plenty of guidance on planning, transition, improvement, even a useful section on cultural change[2]. But it is all provided in the *context* of delivering Services, not of implementing the systems for the delivering of Services. Given the fund of experience built up over twenty years this omission is

---

[1] *Planning to Implement Service Management,* Office of Government Commerce, The Stationery Office, 2002. ISBN-13: 978-0113308774
[2] *Service Transition,* chapter 5

unfortunate and puzzling. Wouldn't want to upset that lucrative consulting industry by issuing a do-it-yourself manual, I guess.

Nevertheless, there is plenty of information in the public domain. Run Google hot for a few hours and an enormous amount of advice can be gleaned – much of it correct. It is beyond the scope of this book (and the expertise of the author) to provide that meta-lifecycle – we simply note it is not in a book... yet.

Here are some broader considerations the IT Skeptic would like to contribute to any collection of advice on how to succeed with ITIL.

Don't do it

No seriously, the easiest way to succeed in an ITIL transformation is not to do it.

Go through these four steps to decide whether it is really a good idea.

All proposed IT projects should be examined on four levels:

- The need/requirement/problem
    - o Is there a good reason to do this?
- The expected return
    - o Is it worth doing? (See "Return on investment", p88)
- Alignment with plans, especially business strategy[1]
    - o Is it the kind of thing we should be focusing on?
- The proposal's place in the project portfolio (you do manage your project portfolio, right?)
    - o The project might pass the preceding tests, but is it the ***best*** (optimal) use of resources? Would the interests of the business be better served by using these funds and people elsewhere?

These criteria apply as much to ITIL as to any IT project. But many ITIL proposals only get assessed to the first one or two

---

[1] The IT Skeptic is an adherent to the school of thought that there should be no such thing as an "IT Strategy": there will be mentions of IT where applicable in the business strategy and IT works to that.

levels, especially if Excessive Technical Fastidiousness (p65) kicks in.

Recommendations

52. Assess all IT proposals to the four levels described above.

53. If it does not pass all four tests, make a management decision whether to proceed regardless but at least you will make it in full understanding of the situation. Naturally the IT Skeptic in general recommends rejecting any proposal that does not meet all four criteria.

Do it as a project

In the last section we said that one does not "do" ITIL. It is important that the transformation is **not** approached as a discrete piece of work that will end and everyone go home, ITIL done.

When we say "You don't 'do' ITIL", we mean don't do it like this, a high rate of expenditure followed by none:

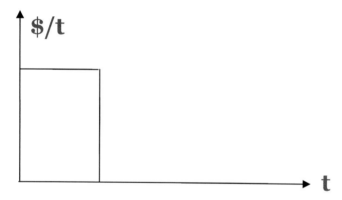

In theory you could introduce an ITIL transformation like this:

i.e. start a Continual Service Improvement Program and work steadily at transforming things at a constant rate of expenditure.

But:

- All ITIL initiatives need initial planning, analysis, design, organisation and promotion in order to overcome organisational inertia and establish momentum.

- In order to show return there need to be some initial quick wins and visible progress.

- And most organisations use a project structure to gate funding.

So the start of an ITIL transformation will always be a project, as should other smaller pieces of work. The reality is that the spend will look like this:

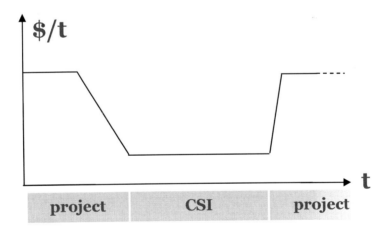

...and it will repeat. In order to merely consolidate and retain what you achieve in the first "push", you will need to do "refreshes" periodically. And if it is really as successful as its proponents said it would be, then you will want to do even more in a second phase right?

Recommendations

54. Make it a formal project: business case, budget, goals, milestones, and PIR[1]. The point here is that if you are going to do it you should do it properly.

55. Don't ask people to transform the processes they use in their spare time. Don't mess about with half-assed tinkering that will always go nowhere.

56. Don't all pack up and go home when it is done: there must be an ongoing program as described in "ITIL is an approach not a project", p113

---

[1] Post Implementation Review

People Process Technology

People Process Technology is a fundamental model for approaching any IT undertaking. (Some ITIL sources add a fourth dimension: Partners[1]. An even more complex model lists vision and strategy, steering, processes, people, technology, and culture[2].)

The key is to start them in that order (People then Process then Technology) and keep them in balance.

IT people too often start with the technology, occasionally start with the process, and seldom start with the people (culture, team, approval, support, enthusiasm...).

Technology works where it is a tool to assist people and support process, where it has been selected or designed to suit those processes and people, and where the people and process can work just as well with or without it.

Technology makes people more efficient and processes more reliable. It seldom makes something possible that was impossible without it.

Put another way, good people can deal with bad process and inadequate tools, and good processes will compensate for inadequate tools; but installing good tools won't fix bad process, and the best processes in the world don't make good people.

My consulting clients get sick of hearing "People Process Technology" from me, but then I get sick of hearing violations of it from some of them.

---

[1] *An Introductory Overview of ITIL*, C. Rudd, itSMF 2004
[2] *Planning to Implement Service Management*, Vernon Lloyd, The Stationery Office, 2002

HOW TO SUCCEED WITH ITIL

Tick the ones you have been guilty of:

- ☐ "Yes but what is the change **form** going to look like?"
- ☐ "I want an out-of-the-box solution"
- ☐ "We are too busy to improve that right now"
- ☐ "We've just bought this service desk and now we need to figure out how to use it"
- ☐ "We thought the processes would come with the tool"
- ☐ "All we need from you is a document"
- ☐ "All we need from you is some forms"
- ☐ "All we need from you is to set up the processes in the tool"
- ☐ "I can't figure out why no-one is following the process we published. Doesn't anyone around here *read*?"
- ☐ "[The vendor] will provide services to install the product, load the sample data, and run one training course"
- ☐ "I can't fire him for not following the process, he's the best technical guy we have"
- ☐ "If we had a better tool than this clunky old thing, people might start to use it"
- ☐ "How can we integrate the processes without integrated tools?"
- ☐ "He doesn't have to go through procurement, he's a GM"
- ☐ "When we decided to introduce Change I didn't realise it would have so much impact"
- ☐ "We did ITIL last year"
- ☐ "We can't afford improvements"

Cultural Change (again)

People first. As discussed, an ITIL project is about transformation not implementation. ITIL is a cultural transformation. It is the change of mindset to a service orientation. It is changing people. By changing the people, we make it possible to change the processes.

This is far and away the most neglected aspect of ITIL projects, (even more than the next factor we discuss: Executive Commitment).

To change attitudes you change behaviour. To change behaviour you change processes and procedures.

To make those changes more efficient you think about introducing technology to meet the gaps, bottlenecks, error-generators and inefficiencies you have found in your procedures.

The work of John Kotter in this area is an excellent approach – the generally accepted one - with his eight-step change model. Any number of authors and consultants are eager to enlighten you, including the ITIL3 *Service Transition* book, which includes it as part of a good introduction to cultural change (chapter 5).

Here are some additional thoughts. Cultural change is about communication, motivation and education.

Communication

Build an inclusive community. Make people feel part of the change; that they have some ownership, some influence, the feeling that their ideas are in it somewhere. Make decisions transparent. Share the rationale, and the process to get to the decision.

Address resistance. Flush it out. Debate. Air grievance. Better to get these things thrashed out than let them fester. Provide an anonymous forum for dissent. Better you know.

Tip: emails are not communication. Workshops, phone calls, discussions, meetings, reviews, and walkthroughs are communication. Newsletters are better than nothing, but best of all is always talking.

Motivation

Encourage, measure and incent. The best way to get people to do something is to pay them to do it. Paid KPIs famously distort behaviour, but well designed ones are better than nothing. Provide feedback, positive and negative. Let people know they are being measured. Show them the results. Hand out praise and glory.

Education

The ITIL sheep-dip (ITIL Foundation training) is not enough. Often it is too much, meaning most people don't actually need it, they need something else.

They need training but not in the theory of ITIL. They need training in how it is going to work applied to their jobs; what they need to do differently, what they own, what they are measured on. That is real ITIL training and it is as rare as hens' teeth.

It greatly concerns me the numbers of people being sent on ITIL Foundation training. Given the cost of ITIL certification, I suggest companies who send staff on theoretical ITIL training - other than the small number actually involved in designing the transformation - are wasting their money. The real target group for that theoretical training are the specialists and consultants.

Use external experts, your own project team and user stakeholders to develop in-house training around :

- why are we doing this?
- what changes for us?
- which of our in-house roles are impacted?
- what do our new procedures look like?
- what will you as an individual need to do differently?
- where can you find the detail of your new procedures?
- what help, support and coaching is available?
- how do you feed back?
- how will we measure and reward this?
- most of all: what's in this for you?

Organisations should do this for two reasons:

1) All the ITIL theory is "just another certificate" to most staff. Yes it creates a few enthusiasts, but the above training will create more. [BTW, the other reason you do ITIL theoretical training is to give your staff a rubber stamp, for their career's sake. Fine, if you understand what you are doing and why.]

2) If they don't do that training anyway the transformation will fail. Such training in what it actually means to the organisation is an utterly essential foundation to cultural change. Without it, all the manuals and flowcharts and new titles are useless.

Many of the training factories are just that: factories. They don't have the skills or procedures to design this kind of custom in-house training - it takes real consulting and business analysis. The consultants working on the transformation are the ones to do it, or training specialists in consultation with them, working with the in-house transformation project team. The value for money is much greater, which is of course what it is all about.

Even good training is not enough either. People remember less than half of what they are taught, and internalise almost none of it. You need:

- repeat/refresher training
- discussions/workshops on how it is going
- assessment: on-the-job observation and measurement
- support: buddying and coaching for those struggling

Why won't IT departments coach? It is that IT machismo thing: "I never had any help. I just grabbed the manuals and jumped in. Think or thwim". The cost and effort of setting up an effective coaching program will be one of the best investments a manager can make.

Tip: manuals are not education.

Sound like hard work? Not as hard as trying to change process without the support of the people.

Sound expensive? At least a third of your investment should be in the people. Aim for half.

This means the overall cost of the project will be higher, right? If the cost of tools is to be a lower proportion then the overall cost must be higher. Consider it as cementing your investment in process and technology. If you don't spend on cultural change, your process and tools work will have been for naught. Either the implementation will fail, or it will go live but later fall into disuse and disrepair. Do it properly. Plan for cultural change, spend for it, and do it as part of the transformational project.

Recommendations

57. Make cultural change the primary goal and success indicator of the project.

58. Don't accept any planning that does not make cultural change its main objective and a large part of its activities.

59. Look at the project spending on activities such as communications, collaboration, workshops, walkthroughs, training, monitoring, coaching, feedback, reviews and celebration. 5% on people is token. 30% is more like it. 50% is getting serious about culture change.

60. Train a few in-house specialists and champions in ITIL theory. In their case, Foundation is not enough. They need some Intermediate too. If they want Expert they are probably leaving you soon :)

61. Rent real expertise from external consultants (because no training course will create in-house experts).

62. Develop in-house training.

63. Monitor the "vibe". There will be resistance. Resistance is not useless – resistance is a positive sign, at least in the early stages. All good sales people know that objections are buying signals. However if resistance continues, and even becomes entrenched, management must take action. Bombard the entrenched positions with training and workshops. In the worst case "if you can't change the people, change the people": get someone who will play nicely.

Executive commitment

Executive commitment is not executive blah-blah. You and your superiors must walk the walk. Warning: this means coming up with money. More importantly, it means making the same cultural change expected of your staff.

This may be as difficult for you as it is for them, so be prepared for the executive to undergo the cultural change program along with the rest of the staff.

And when the rules change, the changes apply to everyone. There is not a ceiling to Change Control: it applies to all levels of management. So too does a standard desktop configuration or hardware purchasing process. No special laptops for the SVP of Marketing. No production changes steamrolled in by the CFO.

If they get away with it, everyone will try.

Recommendations

64. Integrate Service Management into the image and culture of the largest possible unit of the organisation (at best, the company; at least, the Production section of IT).

65. Project a Service Management ethos to clients and expect it from suppliers and partners

66. Get Service Management written into everyone's KPIs. At executive levels too high to influence their KPIs, show them how ITSM delivers on their current KPIs (if it doesn't, you have a problem).

67. There are two ways to deal with executives taking "back doors":

    1) Ensure the CEO is committed to the program and will over-rule them when they try.

    2) Change the rules to make executive privilege transparent. Have a Platinum level of service that permits what they want – make it official.

Resourcing

Don't ask staff to do ITIL part-time, or worse still "spare-time". Create a real project with a professional Project Manager, allocate full-time resource, give it commitment and adequate funding, and ring-fence it.

Don't ask staff to make it up. Buy in expertise to lower the learning curve for your people, and to inject knowledge. Buy in additional head-count just to get the work done and get some momentum.

So outside expertise is essential and all the usual caveats apply. Beware of kids in suits. Many consulting firms have one or two top performing show-ponies who will be there for the presales but nowhere to be found (or jetting in briefly) when the engagement kicks off. That is when the kids in suits arrive.

The ITIL Foundation course is not a qualification for anything other than to understand some of the buzz-speak and sometimes to get them to drink the Kool Aid and get ITIL.

Even an ITIL Expert certification (names vary: in ITIL2 it is called a Manager's or Master's certificate) is only mildly impressive.

Insist on the old warriors with the battle scars – there is no substitute for experience in ITSM.

Recommendations

68. Get consultants.

69. The good local independents are best – use word-of-mouth referrals. Next best are the reputable big firms.

ITIL is an approach not a project

"You don't do ITIL". "Do ITIL as a project with proper project management". "ITIL is an approach not a project". Confused now? Let us clarify.

ITIL is a transformation of the way you do things. The start of such a transformation should be approached as a distinct project, in order for it to get the funding and the focus it requires, and in order to make the right decision about whether it is a good idea. Just drifting into ITIL in people's "spare time" is a bad idea doomed to fail.

On the other hand, treating ITIL as a discrete event with an end is also a mistake, and also doomed to fail. ITIL is not a transformation of technology, nor of process. ITIL, or rather Service Management, is a transformation of culture: of the way people think, of how they approach their jobs. Such cultural change never happens as a result of a brief burst of activity. It requires steady ongoing reinforcement, reminders, monitoring and correction. Otherwise it won't stick.

ITIL talks about Continual Service Improvement (CSI). In fact one of the five core books of Version 3 has that title. But ITIL's thinking in this area is immature, compared to say SPICE or CMM or Six Sigma. Nevertheless the intent is that an initial move towards ITIL alignment is made, followed by a continual process of refinement towards endlessly shifting goals.

What is often overlooked is that this CSI program is not optional. Even if the initial ITIL project has achieved a goodenough state, a continual[1] program is essential just to maintain that current state, to prevent recidivism, to "chock the wheel" of the Deming Cycle, as we discussed in "You don't 'do' ITIL", p61.

Unless ITIL is perceived as "how we do things around here now" it will be just another management fad, just another one of those annoying ideas from on high to be tolerated until it too fades away, like fish or cheese[2].

Make no mistake: ITIL is a cultural transformation, not a process reengineering or – shudder - a tools implementation, although it might involve those.

Recommendations

70. Approach ITIL as a cultural change program.

71. Engage cultural change expertise.

72. Have a budget and resources (and accountability) for the ongoing program after the project "ends".

---

[1] ITIL V3 makes a nice distinction between "continual" and "continuous". A continual program is ongoing but not all the time – it is regular and recurrent.

[2] *FISH!* Lundin, Paul & Christensen, Hyperion 2000, 0786866020
Who Moved My Cheese? Johnson, Vermilion 2002, 0091883768
These are actually really good cultural change ideas, but in the author's experience they are invariably implemented in a burst of enthusiasm and soon forgotten, by management and workers alike.

Integrate

Don't let an ITIL project operate stand-alone, or get all elitist.

The people involved should include stakeholders from development, projects, finance, management, suppliers and HR.

The new processes should re-use existing process wherever possible.

ITIL processes must be linked up with those from other areas of the organisation, for example:

- Business Management

    □ Business strategy and plans

    □ Policy for employee access and provisioning

    □ Continuity policy and planning

    □ Data ownership and policy

    □ Change approval

    □ Service level negotiation

    □ Major incident response

- Project Management

    □ Project portfolio must be included in availability and capacity planning

    □ Evaluation and acceptance criteria must be taken into account from the start of the project and baked into the design

- ☐ Projects should extend beyond go-live into warranty

- ☐ All changes above a certain size should be projects.

- Development

  - ☐ Linking changes with the SDLC[1]

  - ☐ Tracking progress, including test results

  - ☐ Operational acceptance

  - ☐ Releasing into production

- Procurement

  - ☐ Awareness of new assets should be automatic

  - ☐ It may be unnecessary for IT to track any financial or supplier information

- Human Resources

  - ☐ Employee moves, add, changes.

  - ☐ New employee notification to IT, and their role or profile, should be automatic

  - ☐ Likewise employee change of role, or departure

  - ☐ Employee contact information should be centrally administered

  - ☐ Inform and educate on policies (security, process, change...)

---

[1] Software Development LifeCycle: the control system for builds, versioning, review, approval, and migration between environments of source code. I think I'm showing my age with this term but what do I know about Development?

□ Service and asset provisioning (should be managed by HR or IT but not both)

- Vendor/supplier

    □ Interface to their support processes and systems

    □ Contract negotiations (informed by SLAs)

Recommendations

73. Ensure the ITIL project is properly integrating with the rest of the organisation: check workshop attendees, trainee lists, design sign-offs.

ITIL2 vs. ITIL3

Don't leap into ITIL3. The vendors will want you to, but it is a big step until some sort of staged methodology exists. For those organisations that feel they have "conquered' ITIL2, version 3 is a logical next step. But for organisations starting out, it can appear an inaccessibly advanced goal.

People are starting to realise how different ITIL3 ("The Refresh") is from ITIL2, and how much more extensive the scope and ideas are. There is no doubt that the re-engineering has been extensive. A bit like a DOS-based command-line-driven utility being rewritten as a Windows GUI with workflow. The original routines are still in there but the manuals sure look different! Saying it is an add-on is like saying a Chevrolet Corvette is an add-on to a V8 motor, or Windows is an add-on to MS-DOS. Sure ITIL2 is still in there somewhere but not so as you'd notice.

For organisations starting out, unless you are one of a small minority of state-of-the-art service providers, my advice is to go for ITIL2, for now.

- There is nothing much wrong with ITIL2

- ITIL3 is too big with little help available (yet) on getting there - no sign of any complementary guidance about the path to ITIL - the meta-lifecycle – yet (early 2009)

- ITIL3 is too raw and nobody understands it properly yet; certainly not the Service Strategy book ☺

- ITIL3 certification isn't even finished yet, and

- Only a small proportion of the ITIL community are advanced enough to need ITIL3

ITIL2 works. It's good. The IT Skeptic has been critical of aspects of ITIL2 but overall it is a fine body of knowledge. If one just considers the "red and blue books" of ITIL2, then it is well-understood, proven, simpler, less ambitious and more focused on IT service delivery than ITIL3.

If ITIL2 worked for a business last year, why wouldn't it work this year?

As a comment on the itSMFI forum[1] said:

> ITIL is not like software, it is not simply 'new and improved' ... V2 has not lost any of its value with the introduction of V3.

My home PC is a Pentium 3. It runs SimCity 3 which is all I ask. My phone is an old i-Mate PocketPC: a big chunky slab, no fancy keyboards, no 3G, no WiFi. For many years I drove a 1974 Holden HQ Kingswood. That will mean something to only a tiny minority of readers, but if I tell you it had a bench front seat and a three-on-the-tree column shift, you'll get the idea.

These "old" technologies work. They met the business requirement back then so why not now? Sometimes the requirements move on and so must the supporting infrastructure but sometimes they don't. Or the move can be delayed until the infrastructure is ready.

Not only does ITIL2 work well, but ITIL3 is a big ask. If ITIL2 taught us how to walk, ITIL3 teaches us how to run. The trouble is many organisations are still sitting down. Only some organisations have already embarked on the ITIL journey and many are not that far along the road. Maybe only 10% of ITIL adopters are ready to make use of the more advanced aspects of ITIL3.

---

[1] Michiel Croon, www.itsmfi-forum.org

Certainly there is an attraction in starting out with ITIL3 so you don't need to "convert" later. Do not rush into this decision.

ITIL is about improving maturity step by step. ITIL3 is a maturing of ITIL over ITIL2. We are endlessly reassured that they are upwardly compatible. So stick with ITIL2 for now.

Some organisations make a policy of waiting for "service pack 1" of anything — the first wave of fixes (which we have in fact quietly had already for ITIL3, not that anyone will have told you, there is no public release management for ITIL). Actually ITIL3 looks remarkably clean for such a major rewrite, a tribute to all the editing and review, so this is not a compelling argument for delay.

More importantly, if you hold out for a while then we hope to see more complementary guidance books published to extend and elaborate on the core books. Especially one would hope to see more guidance on how to get from here to there – how to implement ITIL.

As a result of integrating all the "Lost Books" of ITIL2 (how many know that there are nine or 11 books in ITIL2?), ITIL3 is an order of magnitude broader and more complex than the "red and blue books" of ITIL2. This is an advance for the industry, a step up in competency.

Unfortunately it is only a step up if you are already standing on the ITIL2 step. If you have not embarked on the service management journey yet, then ITIL3 represents a high wall. Chuck the five ITIL3 books at a beginner and they'd run screaming.

ITIL3 provides no intermediate steps up the wall. ITIL2 is the only "beginner's ITIL" available. OGC[1] and TSO[2] are hell-bent on killing off ITIL2 as fast as possible. But ITIL2 will not go away easily until something like an *ITIL for Dummies* comes out as part of ITIL3 complementary guidance. Or people will start turning to simpler alternatives such as FITS[3].

The other book we desperately need is *How to Implement ITIL3* providing a progressive series of steps up that wall. The current five core books say where to get to but they still say little about how to get there. Wait until something gets published that does.

Most important of all, you should wait for consensus to emerge about what works and what doesn't in ITIL3. Sadly ITIL3 has a bet each way: it is a mix of proven guidance and bleeding edge thought-leadership. A better term than "best practice" is "good practice" and an even better term is "generally accepted practice", like GAAP for accountants. Either ITIL is Generally Accepted Service Management Practice or it is providing thought-leadership for where ITSM should be going in the future. It says it is the former, and everyone thinks it is, but it behaves as if it is either, depending on the author and the chapter.

There are no clear indicators in the books of which ideas are which. They should be colour coded; green for safe proven GASMP; blue for blue-sky theoretical ideas suggested to the industry as a future direction (at least one of the books could just be printed on blue paper). But they aren't.

---

[1] UK's Office of Government Commerce, "owners" of ITIL

[2] The Stationery Office, formerly the UK Government printers and now a privatized for-profit organisation. The official publishers of ITIL.

[3] Online content at becta.org.uk/fits/index.cfm, or for a book read *FITS pocket guide*, Becta, Becta, 2004. publications.becta.org.uk/display.cfm?resID=25868

This is dangerous for the very people ITIL is supposed to serve: those who need guidance in ITSM. If you know enough ITSM to differentiate when ITIL is being pragmatic and when it is being blue sky, then you don't need the books. So wait until there is a clearer picture of the safe and not so safe zones of ITIL3.

Wait for the consultants to have a bit more than a two-day "upgrade" course under their belts. Heck, at this rate all the exams won't be ready until 2009, so where are you going to get an ITIL3 master anyway? By end of 2009 he or she may know what they are talking about.

For the great majority of readers, you don't need to go ITIL3 in 2009. Come 2010 or later, you will have made enough progress in some of your ITIL disciplines to actually consider the next maturity step, to ITIL3.

Recommendations

74. For the average site, if you are starting out on the ITIL road, look to ITIL2 "red and blue books" as the map, or if you have good consultants then mix and match ITIL2 with a few of the better elements of ITIL3, such as Request Fulfilment, Event Management, Service Evaluation and Service Portfolio.

75. Wait for ITIL3 to mature and for consultants to get some experience. Wait at least until 2010.

76. If you are already an ITIL shop, or you are an advanced site in need of all that ITIL3 holds, then by all means consider the case for stepping up to ITL3 – it offers a lot.

Do a Service Catalogue early

The Service Catalogue documents all of the services provided to the users, along with the Service Levels agreed in the Service Level Agreement or SLA. See "Service Catalogue", p90, for our four-level model of Service Catalogue. Here we are talking about the Current Catalogue, what the person-in-the-street understands as Service Catalogue.

Regardless of which ITIL processes are being addressed first, a Current Catalogue must come very early in the project, to give people a framework for subsequent efforts, and just as importantly to provide a touchstone to drive service-centric thinking into the staff culture.

This does not always happen in practice. There is a school of thought that one should not attempt a Service Catalogue until you can define and measure what you are capable of delivering. This attitude arises from "Catalogue" being used to refer to all four types of catalogue discussed in "Service Catalogue", p90. A Technical Catalogue and the associated SLAs should definitely wait until we can specify what is feasible in the SLAs. Likewise it might be unwise to provide a Current Catalogue to users and customers before then.

But a Current Catalogue is essential early in the project to provide focus for IT staff. If you can position it properly and set expectations with customers, then it also provides a sound basis for discussions with them too, so long as they understand that the SLA part comes later.

Ideally, a first draft of the Brochure Catalogue should also come fairly soon after, as a sketch of what providers and customers would like the services to be, in order to define what we are working towards.

Recommendations

77. Ensure the Current Catalogue is an early planned deliverable. Don't let the perfectionists hold out for more information or a clearer picture – get a Current Catalogue out to your IT staff as soon as possible, if only as a basis for debate.

78. Ensure the Current Catalogue is a keystone of the communications plan.

Restrain Configuration Management

IT people seem fixated with "one ring to rule them all" solutions: relational database, corporate data model, data-dictionary, repository, executive information systems, dashboard, portal, middleware, directory, and SOA. Getting everything in one place appeals to our tidy minds, but history shows the effort is usually not cost effective and falls short of the ideal mark.

Configuration Management is very appealing in concept: have a process that gathers together information about all the objects managed by IT and their inter-relationships; and provide views into the data so that staff can walk the relationships to understand the impacts (ideally the business service impacts) of changes or outages. The repository of all this data is the CMDB (see "CMDB can not be done", p68).

Make sure those working on ITIL understand the distinction between Configuration Management the process and CMDB the technology. You need Configuration Management the process. You do it now, at some level of maturity. People keep this data in their heads, in spreadsheets, in databases, inside tools.

Understand what level of maturity you need to get to with Configuration Management the process, and how critical it is to your organisation that you can access the data and how quickly you need it.

Only then can you decide whether you need to implement a CMDB.

Probably all companies that actually manage to get something working (many don't) will then benefit from CMDB. The real question is whether the benefit justifies the cost (often not) and whether it was the best use of the funds (usually not). For a small proportion of companies who are very complex or for whom IT is really critical, CMDB pays off.

CMDB appeals to the technoid's desire for a technical fix to a cultural and procedural problem. Sadly, technology does not fix process.

The IT Skeptic has seriously proposed[1] an alternative approach to keeping all the Configuration data centralised and current: assemble as much of it as you need *on demand* in response to a requirement.

Consider if we created the configuration data when we needed it in response to some particular situation instead of trying to maintain all the data all the time in a CMDB.

This is nothing new; it is what we do now. We create data ad-hoc anyway when we have to. If the data is not there or not right and management wants the report, we gather it up and clean it up and present it just in time, trying not to look hot and bothered and panting.

How much better if we had a team, expert in producing on-demand configuration information? They would have formal written procedures for accessing, compiling, cleaning and verifying data, which they would practice and test. They would have tools on the ready and be trained in using them. Most of all they would "have the CMDB in their heads": they would know where to go and who to ask to find the answers, and they would have prior experience in how to do that and

---

[1] See *On Demand CMDB*, on the *Owning ITIL* website at www.itskeptic.org/owningitil

what to watch out for. Instead of ad-hoc amateurs responding to a crisis, experts would assemble on-demand data as a business-as-usual process.

They would understand basic statistical sampling techniques. When management wants a report on the distribution of categories of incidents, they would sample a few hundred incidents, categorise them properly according to what the requirements are this time (after all how often does an existing taxonomy meet the needs of a new management query?) and respond accordingly.

They would be an on-call team, responsive to emergency queries. "The grid computing system has died and the following servers are not dynamically reconfiguring. Which services are impacted and which business owners do we call on a Saturday?" They may not know the answers off the top of their heads but they will know - better than just about anyone - where and how to look to get the answers, and how long that is going to take.

They would have formal written procedures for accessing, compiling, cleaning and verifying data, which they would practice and test. They would have tools on the ready and training in using them. Most of all they would have the CMDB in their heads: they would know where to go and who to ask to find the answers, and they would have prior experience in how to do that and what to watch out for. Instead of ad-hoc amateurs responding to a crisis, on-demand data would be a business-as-usual process.

Certainly we would need some basic CMDB data kept continually. This would be the stuff we discover automagically already, such as procurement-driven asset databases, or auto-discovered network topologies and desktop inventories, or the transactional information captured by the Service Desk. Add to that the stuff we document on paper already (or ought to): change records, the service catalogue, phone lists, contracts and so on.

The savings in not trying to go beyond that base CMDB data would be great. The price paid for those savings would be that "on-demand" does not mean "instantaneous". It might mean hours or days or even weeks to respond to the demand. So a business analysis needs to be done to find out how current the data really needs to be (as compared to what the technical perfectionists say). In some organisations the criticality demands instant data and they need to trudge off down the CMDB path. But for the majority of organisations this just isn't so.

Recommendations

79. Severely limit your Configuration scope.

80. For most sites (except those aiming for maturity 4 or 5 Configuration Management, such as NASA or Boeing or EDS or Tata), don't do a CMDB.

81. Have a "CMDB called Sue": two or more humans tasked with knowing the configuration of your environment and being available as impact analysis experts.

82. Encourage the use of out-of-the-box CMDB tool solutions, however imperfect, rather than in-house developed systems.

83. For preference, the CMDB – if you must have one - should be an integrated part of the Service Desk tool, not a separate product, i.e. buy the integration – don't do it yourself.

84. Stamp out attempts to implement a complete idealised by-the-book ITIL CMDB unless yours is a very large organisation with perfectionist standards or critical requirements, and deep pockets.

85. If there really is a business case for full CMDB, do not lay the burden of maintaining the data on a central team. Ensure all groups responsible for the development, maintenance and operation of services are required and incented to take responsibility for "their" data in the CMDB. Do however have an owner of the CMDB responsible for maintenance, audit and reporting.

86. If you don't need a CMDB, then focus on network configuration ("what is connected to what"), asset data ("what is what"), and device inventory ("what runs on what").

87. Consider "on-demand CMDB", a team, expert in producing on-demand configuration information.

Tools

IT people are typically drawn to the industry because they like technical things. They are object-oriented people, and not in the programming sense. While there is a significant minority who like process (often project managers or ITIL consultants), the majority don't.

As a result, we tend to start with the technology, and build a whole solution around tools. This is a mistake. For almost all problems that IT sets out to solve, the technology doesn't really matter.

They all work

Tools don't work. Not for what many people ask them to do: to fix a problem. Install your tools, maybe even design a process around them, but it will fail. It might take one year to fail or three but it will fail. Start with the people, change the culture/mindset/habits/attitude, and then help those people look at process. Once process requirements *in your organisation* are understood, find a tool to fit. Any other sequence is imposing a change on a culture that has not accepted it and is therefore doomed. So in usual exaggerated fashion, the IT Skeptic says "tools don't matter".

Tools don't matter for another reason: they all work. Tools work for what people often **don't** ask them to do, which is to provide some efficiency and reliability to existing healthy processes.

If a tool doesn't work **at all**, even the most inept product evaluation should discover that and the vendor will soon be out of business.

Recommendations

88. Get the process right, then shortlist tools that fit, and then any of the tools will be adequate. Sure, some will be better than others, but they'll all do the job. Buy on vendor and price.

89. When assessing fit, ensure that vendor credibility, financial stability, local support, and price all receive sufficient weight – don't let the geeks obsess on features.

90. Don't overlook open source and software-as-a-service (SaaS) options.

Process drives requirements

We are drawn to IT by a fascination with complex technology. This is unfortunate because it blinds many of us to the importance of the People Process Technology trilogy.

The order is important: People come first. IT folk too often start with the technology, occasionally start with the process, and seldom start with the people.

Once we understand what will and won't work culturally and what we need to do to get there, only then are we in a position to design and implement processes (unless of course you like doing it several times, or failing). There is no best practice, only generally agreed practice. So no definition of process is sacred; they all need to adapt to the receiving organization.

The link between People and Practice is education: inform, train, coach.

So Practice/Process comes after People. It follows naturally. It must be said that not everyone sees it this way: "data design comes before coding"; "buy a tool and let it dictate the process"; "a good repository is the starting point"; "you can't do anything until you have acquired some data".

There is an interesting debate in IT between action-oriented thinking and object-oriented (we are talking more generally than the programming-related meanings here). Here is a crude linguistic test for process orientation or technology orientation: do they talk about verbs/actions or nouns/things?

The data/process, technology/process, objects/activities, nouns/verbs arguments are like the nature/nurture one: The reality is somewhere in the middle as both are important. The culture of IT as the first decade of the millennium heads to a close is off-balance, object-centric. IT gets more complex and unstable every day. If you listen to the vendors, apparently the solution is not to look at how we do things and the quality and culture of the people doing them. No, it is to introduce yet more technology.

There is a point, well into the process design, when we identify opportunities for tools to help manage the process and in some cases even help automate the process. Once we understand our people's capabilities and desires, once we understand exactly what we want the process to do, then yes, we may build a solid business case to buy a tool.

In order to select the tool, we need to understand what we have to achieve with each transaction, and how we plan to perform the transaction. So you need to be well advanced down the process design path before you start selecting tools. Personally I would wait until the processes have been tested in walkthroughs, but you can only hold the geeks off for so long. The main thing is not to let them start the project by looking at tools.

Most business issues that IT addresses are culture or process problems. If you have a cultural problem, there is not a technology solution. If you are paunchy and aging, buying a red sports car does not fix the problem (though you may feel better about it). Technology works where it is a tool to assist people and support process, where it has been selected or designed to suit those processes and people, and where the people and process work with or without it. Technology makes people more efficient and processes more reliable. It seldom makes something possible that was impossible without it.

In the PPT model, the term "Things" might be better than "Technology" because the fixation is more general: with products, documentation, forms..., all kinds of objects. You even find people treating process as a thing (stay with me here). To implement new practices you need to look at the people doing the implementation, and the process for implementing the process (the "meta-process"?), before you capture the process as a document.

Yet some projects start by designing the forms, then work out how the forms will function. Sometimes organizations do nothing but post a form and declare a new process is in place. It is the same old Things-first thinking. And they fail. The forms sit unused.

Likewise we see projects where the process was written up as a document and distributed, and that was the implementation. Once again, they fail. The documents gather dust. Look around: how many process flowcharts hang on walls or sit on shared drives or in binders on shelves without having any instantiation in reality?

People Process Technology. People Practices Things. Whatever the model, please consider the culture first and the things last, and you will find implementations of new services, systems, practices and software go so much better.

Recommendations

91. Ensure all tool implementations start from cultural change, from people, improvement, and move forward from there into process and things.

92. Don't try to fix people with technology.

ITIL compliance

The OGC and itSMF let down their constituencies when they ignored the whole area of product compliance. There is no official definition of ITIL product compliance.

Suddenly every vendor has ITIL. Most IT operational tools claim to "support ITIL" or to be "ITIL compliant." One vendor announced they are seeking "ITIL certification," no less (only individuals can be certified, not products or suppliers or user organisations).

The infuriating ones are those that map ITIL keywords to discrete features of their product; with varying degrees of compliance with the actual meaning of the word: "Oooh! Oooh! IT Continuity. We do that. The administrator can do a backup of our product's data."

ITIL is technology-agnostic. You can do ITIL with Post-it™ notes, and the way things are going it won't be long before 3M are advertising Post-it notes as "ITIL compliant."

Vendors are full of it when it comes to ITIL. It is far too easy to slap the word "ITIL" on an operations tool. This only serves to debase what ITIL means and to confuse the community.

You can sympathize with the vendors (as much as one can). They can hardly ignore ITIL, yet OGC and itSMF both let an opportunity slip by when they ignored product compliance. No doubt they had good reasons for standing aloof from the whole sordid business but they have left unregulated an area that cries out for some control.

Today, there is no formal independent certification of ITIL compliance for tools. Pink Elephant provides PinkVerify™ commercial licensed certification but, in the IT Skeptic's experience, this is not a good indicator of compliance with some of the criteria below.

OGC set up individual professional certification early on, and now finally ISO/IEC has given us organisational certification (the 20000 standard). There are rumours of possible ISO20000 product compliance criteria in future. The product vendors have no choice but to make their own claims, and nowhere to go other than Pink Elephant to verify them in the event their claims are in fact correct.

But there are some obvious criteria for a reasonable person's definition of "ITIL compliant." Ask your prospective vendor these questions about their supposedly ITIL-compliant or ITIL-supporting tool (including some PinkVerified ones):

Who says it is compliant or that it supports ITIL? On what basis? To what maturity and in what capabilities?

Just because they think it supports Incident Management at maturity Level 2 is of little relevance if you need Service Level Management at maturity 4.

How many of their product designers are certified ITIL Managers or Experts?

Is the chief product architect certified? If none, then who are the ITIL masters who consult on design? Ask for a conference call with their ITIL designers to discuss compliance.

Does it use ITIL terminology (correctly)?

Part of the benefit of any standard framework is standard terms, so that new staff, service providers, auditors, trainers and contractors can all quickly understand your organisation and communicate clearly. So it is not OK if an incident is called something other than an incident (especially if an incident is called a problem and a problem is called a fault). Confusion will be endless.

Does it implement ITIL processes out of the box?

Just because your vendor uses ITIL terminology that still does not mean they support ITIL. The ITIL processes are clearly defined in the books. If it doesn't work to these processes (and the wide range of the variants that arise at implementation) it doesn't support ITIL. It is too easy to change the words on a few screens and declare compliance.

Pretty much every one of the larger players provides consulting services to implement their tool in an ITIL environment, but check what comes as standard implementation services: does it include ITIL procedures or workflows? Some don't even mention ITIL.

Check what is in the manuals and on their website. If there is hardly a mention of ITIL then you know their service guys have the tough job of putting lipstick on a pig.

Does the tool support workflow?

(...pretty odd if a process-compliant tool doesn't). Does it come with pre-defined workflow for the "standard" ITIL procedures (clearly flowcharted in the ITIL2 red book and blue book)? How does the documentation explain implementing the workflow in support of ITIL process?

Since ITIL is all about quality management, how does their tool supports this out-of-the-box? For instance, how does it support determining quality targets? How does it measure and report improvement over time? Does it explicitly implement a Deming Cycle (Plan, Do, Check, Act) in the tool? Note: just about every product in the market fails this one.

Does the tool consolidate information to a service view?

Tools that cannot measure and communicate in terms of a service are not ITIL tools (though they can provide a foundation of data for ITIL tools).

For example, a monitoring tool should show current status of a service; a Service Desk should show the current view of a service based on incidents, problems and changes; a Service Desk and/or SLA tool should provide historical reporting of consolidated availability information and cumulative statistics by service.

How does it support SLAs?

Service Management is nothing without Service Level Management. Regardless of whether it is a tool for Availability, Capacity, Service Desk, Configuration, whatever ... ask them how it is SLA-aware and how it contributes to the monitoring and reporting of SLAs.

SLAs are multi-item written contracts. The contract defines who it is with, what period, who are the key people, what the vertical escalation path is. Each SLA item, known as a Service Level Target or SLT, can define support response times, time-to-repair, percentage availability, performance, resource usage, etc.

Setting a threshold time in which an Incident should be picked up or closed or whatever is not an SLA. It is one SLT that might form part of an SLA if it could be defined on a per-customer basis. Do not allow vendors to redefine the term SLA to suit their own purposes[1].

---

[1] For more on this, see *ABC Cafeterias* on the Owning ITIL website, at www.itskeptic.org/owningitil

SLAs relate to a service. This may seem obvious, but SLAs are not related to an asset or anything else: they define the levels for the service. One individual SLT within an SLA might relate to a metric for an individual asset. SLAs don't.

How many of their field implementation staff or partners have certification beyond ITIL Foundation?

Foundation "sheep-dipping" is a basic process. It provides just enough knowledge to be dangerous (I should know, being a Foundation-level practitioner myself).

If your organization is of any size or complexity, you probably want more highly trained people, although you should look at the broader skills and experience of the individuals involved – the certifications alone don't prove anything. Nevertheless, their overall level of training is at least a measure of their genuine commitment to ITIL.

The big vendors generally excel here (but see next section, "Get tools services"). The small players often pay lip service. Or worse they have no field support at all beyond one product tech at the local distributor. ITIL is about process not tools: you need process people on the ground to help you implement it.

Recommendations

93. If you are going to do ITIL, look for vendors who have real understanding of ITIL, tools that really were designed with ITIL in mind, and a local capability to deliver on an ITIL framework.

Get tools services

Some vendors see ITIL as answering client demand for procedures: "we don't have to provide processes because ITIL does". They confuse process (which ITIL describes) with procedures (which are specific to the tool and the site). Some of them are smart enough to see the revenue opportunities of process consulting, but many don't: they might offer some basic ITIL training, or no services at all.

Therefore for many tools the "services" are just product installation (perhaps customisation) and product training. This is allowed to happen for two reasons:

1) sales hacks. So many IT sales people are ignorant hustlers who barely manage to grasp the main concepts of the technology and only know how to sell something that comes in a box. Selling services is all too complicated and ITIL is just a word.

2) product-fixated clients. Let's not heap all the blame on the vendors. Too many customers want to "buy an ITIL". They don't want the effort of setting up process and they don't want to pay more than the sticker price on the technology.

The result is that the customer's staff poke around modifying the tool without a good idea what they are doing, reinventing procedures and breaking the tool as they struggle over a learning curve they should never have to face alone.

If the right consultants are brought in, they bring knowledge of the tool, proven work procedures, and the right methodologies to work out the processes and the people.

The IT industry seems doomed to forever rediscover that buying IP[1] is cheaper than inventing it.

Get real. The cost of good consulting services to implement a tool will exceed the licence cost of the tool. Such implementation should include devising the work procedures specific to your organisation in collaboration with your staff, and then training all relevant staff in those procedures, documenting them, and setting up an ongoing program to ensure the procedures are monitored and measured and taught to new people in those roles.

Get even more real. That total cost of the tool (software plus services) should be less than a third of the total cost of the project, with the remainder going on modifying processes, and – we say it again – cultural change of the people.

Find the right people. Sometimes the tools vendors have good consultants who are more than product hacks, but they are a minority.

Usually the big consulting firms have good IP and strong people but these get diluted in the field: the good people are supplemented by "kids in suits". Watch out for those "show-pony" experts who only turn up at the start or occasionally.

Often the most experienced and skilled consultants are freelancers who get business by word of mouth. On the other hand anyone can hang up a consultant's shingle.

ITIL qualifications mean little. ITIL3 exams are all multi-choice, there is no practical testing or peer review or ongoing certification, and the courses run in a few days each. There is no substitute for proven results. Even experience doesn't count for much: there are old duffers such as your author who have been banging about the ITSM industry since the

---

[1] Intellectual property

days of MVS mainframes – that does not necessarily make them good ITIL consultants (though it may do).

Dig into a consultant's past. Find out what they have delivered and what the real outcomes were.

Recommendations

94. Get the right amount of money in order to ensure a proper return on the investment in the tool.

95. Spend that money on people who will get the job done right and quickly.

96. Select individual people not the organisations they work for.

97. Select those people based on references: they are only as good as what they have delivered to someone else.

98. Look for a standard package of services: if they have enough experience they should be able to define what they provide.

What tools?

The level of maturity, complexity and criticality of your ITIL processes will make a big difference in your tool requirements, but some generic observations can be made about a minimum set of tools.

Service Desk

In theory a spreadsheet will do but in reality everyone needs a tool that tracks "tickets": incidents problems and changes. They should all be separate entities, not just different codes on a generic ticket record.

Never mind what the vendors tell you: a call- or incident- or work-order-logging system is not a Service Desk system, though a Service Desk should track history: what happened when, and all contacts with people, especially the end user.

It should store asset information and link them to tickets.

It should know about users and link tickets to them. Linking assets to them is good.

Tickets must be able to be passed around between staff, preferably in groups such as Level 1 Support.

A knowledge-base is pretty important: the ability to capture solutions for re-use by end-users and technical staff.

Workflow is nice: the ability to define the standard series of steps that various types of incidents, problems and changes should go through, e.g. change approval.

Asset management

The best place for Asset Management is integrated in the Service Desk tool but you may have a specialised tool to monitor vendor performance, leases etc

CMDB

Enough said elsewhere. It is unlikely that you need full-blown CMDB, so long as

- Service Desk has assets

- Network management can discover and view the network

- Procurement and contractuals are tracked somewhere

- Current Service Catalogue lists key servers and databases

Event Management

If you don't have a message console for event management, centrally monitoring your servers, networks, storage, databases and other key objects, you need one.

It should issue alerts to someone somewhere.

A nice-to-have is automated opening of incident tickets in the Service Desk tool.

End user experience

The quickest, most effective and cheapest way to measure availability (and performance) is with some sort of agent technology on selected desktops, measuring response times of key transactions, reporting the end user experience. Make this an early priority for infrastructure monitoring tools.

Service Catalogue

A text editor will do for Service Catalogue – don't get sold on fancy tools that only constrain your formatting options.

Project Management

Don't try to do Project Management in a Service Desk tool. Use proper PM tools. There are free ones, both online[1] and downloadable[2].

Source code management

Source code management is usually a worthwhile investment. Operations and Development are both stakeholders.

Development may only see a need for version and build management. Full lifecycle management requires release packaging and controlled migration between all environments including the test ones and production.

Reporting

Nearly every IT shop has some sort of generic reporting tool. You want to be able to take data from all the above tools and massage it into service level reporting. (And if you can't, don't promise reporting as a deliverable in SLAs).

---

[1] e.g. Basecamp www.basecamphq.com
[2] e.g. Open Workbench www.openworkbench.org

Recommendations

99. Keep it simple. Unless tools are significantly automating process or increasing the efficiency or effectiveness of process, they serve only to increase cost and risk and time.

100. Integration isn't what it cracked up to be except in the most advanced of sites. Don't sweat it, so long as incident, problem, change, assets and users have some level of linkage.

IT is a customer of IT

It is a constant source of amazement that IT departments treat their own tools with a cavalier disregard.

It is easily argued that monitoring and service desk tools are at least as important as core business systems, and they are probably more so.

If the Service Desk or the central console is unavailable, the implication for the other production systems is obvious, so why are these tools so often NOT given production status?

So they should be treated with the same respect: specifically they should be subject to SLAs and given all the support and priority of any other production system.

Recommendations

101. All IT tools should be in the Service Catalogue as part of services provided by IT to IT, as well as in the Availability and Continuity plans.

102. All tools should have multiple environments: at a minimum test, training and production.

103. All tools should be subject to the same change control as business systems.

104. All critical tools (at least the service desk; the monitoring console; and the network, server and storage monitors) should have designated Level 1 and 2 support personnel, and a "business" owner.

And so on, just as any other service.

Conclusion

("Postface"? "Sufface"?)

ITIL is a good idea when it is a good idea. Sadly there is a wave of hype around ITIL which means that many ITIL-based proposals are not a good idea. The vendors won't tell you, nor will every consultant. Caveat emptor is seen as an ethical waiver in the IT industry.

The ITIL books are full of good ideas. They are not holy writ. Nor are they prescriptive[1]; a lot of work is required to figure out if and how they apply to your organisation.

ITIL is not magic. It is just a tool, to be used along with other tools as part of your transformation of your service processes and culture.

Culture. It is all about the people. If you don't start with the people and focus on the people and spend a large part of the money and effort on the people, then all the process and technology are for naught. But then that is true of any organisational initiative.

> If you enjoyed the ideas in this book, you can find more, along with robust debate over them, at www.itskeptic.org.

---

[1] ITIL does not claim to be prescriptive. On the contrary, the books and the evangelists stress the need to adopt and adapt.

14 questions to ask about an

ITIL project

proposal

1. What is the vision? What is the strategy to achieve that vision?

2. What is the driving need or requirement?

3. How will success be measured? Relative to what benchmark measured now? Are we measuring with something other than ITIL? (See p63) Do the metrics measure the benefits stated in the business case?

4. What process maturity level(s) is the objective? (see p61)

5. Where is the value? Will it reduce costs, increase customer satisfaction, reduce risk, increase competitiveness or what? What dollar value can you put on that? Based on what metrics and where do they come from? Where is the real money?

6. Why do we need this? What is broken? (See p65) Do we really need best practice? Can we go for something simpler? (See p44) In particular is there a CMDB proposed? Why do we need it? (See p68) What does it give us over how it is done now? What pain or risk does it address? Weighed against that, what proportion of the costs is it? Does that include ongoing maintenance and audit of the data?

7. What resistance to this is there? Sometimes there is a good reason for resistance. Go ask the objectors.

8. What proportion of the budget is allocated to people-related activity: cultural change, training...? (See p105)

9. Where are the people resources coming from? People cannot do ITIL in their "spare time". And the people doing this should not all be learning how as they go: make sure some external expertise is being brought in.

10. Who did the estimates (risk, time and cost)? What is their practical experience of doing this same thing before? Does that translate to this situation? Process change and cultural change are even more chronically underestimated than projects are in general, especially when estimated by technical people.

11. What ongoing activities will ensure the implemented changes stick, and that improvement continues over time? Who will own that? How will it be funded? See p105)

12. How does this integrate with other methodologies in use in our organisation? (See p115) ...and other processes currently in place (e.g. procurement, project management, security, hires and fires, facilities)?

13. Have you chosen the tools yet? If so, throw it back. Tools come much later after process requirements are well understood. Technology driven projects usually fail.

14. Do the CEO and CIO support this strongly? If not what makes you think you can change that? No solid executive support = no hope.

This is not an exhaustive list, just suggestions. Check the *Owning ITIL* webpage at www.itskeptic.org/owningitil to see if we have grown or revised this list, and to provide your own feedback so we can.

14 questions to check on progress of an
ITIL project

1. Have you encountered resistance? (Resistance is good). How have you / will you overcome that? (*Ignored resistance is bad*)

2. What champions have you 'converted' to the cause, who weren't on board at the beginning?

3. What cultural change activities have you conducted: workshopping, communications (newsletters etc), consultation, walkthroughs, training, coaching, monitoring, feedback, celebration? NB. Emails don't count as communication

4. Who has been involved and how, from Development, Operations, Testing, Project Management, Architects, Finance, Business Managers, HR?

5. How are you socialising new processes? (emails and posting to websites don't count)

6. In Kotter[1] terms, who is your "guiding coalition"?

7. Have we reviewed the decision to use ITIL as a basis? Have we looked at any other options? (COBIT, MOF, FITS, ISO20000... See p34)

8. How is executive sponsorship holding up? Are all management embracing this? Who is asking for exemptions (e.g. from change approval, or from standard PC models or SOEs)?

---

[1] John Kotter's eight-step change model. Google it.

9. Show me the Service Catalogue (it should exist from early in the project, at least the Current services, see p123).

10. Are we documenting all adaptations, variations and exceptions to "standard" ITIL, with their rationale? (Adaptation is good, so long as it is tracked and the rationale captured)

11. To what extent are we duplicating or replacing existing process?   Was the option canvassed to incorporate existing process instead?   What compromises were involved and why were they rejected?

12. What are customers asking for? Have we documented that as a Brochure catalogue? (see p123) How much of that can we deliver? How much can we measure?

13. Have you identified the need for any new technology? On what basis? (Technical requirements should derive from identified process improvements – see p133). Do the   vendor's   implementation   services   include implementing our new procedure workflows? (See p136) What customisation of tools is required?   (every customisation should be resisted and justified – they add greatly to future maintenance costs)

14. Is the steering committee still active and involved? What don't you want the steering committee to know?

This is not an exhaustive list, just suggestions. Check the *Owning ITIL* webpage at www.itskeptic.org/owningitil to see if we have grown or revised this list, and to provide your own feedback so we can.

14 questions for a

post-ITIL-
implementation
review

1. How has this changed the way people think, speak and act? Describe instances/anecdotes.

2. What has been the feedback from customers? Suppliers?

3. How did we measure success? Did we measure against something other than ITIL? Did we succeed?

4. What has been re-scoped, deferred or dropped since the business case?

5. Are we measuring the ROI? When will we review again to check that we got the ROI expected in the business case?

6. Who owns each and every process? One person per process. Do those people agree they are the owner?

7. Do we have procedure guides for each job role? How does each person know what is expected of them, what has changed in their world and how that impacts them? What KPIs do they have? Are we measuring those? What incentives do they have to meet those KPIs?

8. Where is the process documentation? How is it accessed? Who knows it is there? Who owns it and keeps it current? How much use is it getting?

9. What tools were implemented? Are they treated as production systems? (See p148)

10. Have we documented all adaptations, variations and exceptions to "standard" ITIL?

11. **Most important of all**: What processes are in place to consolidate and protect the investment made? Are we monitoring and reviewing and auditing process compliance? Process quality? Process subversion? (See p105) Are we doing regular skills refreshes? Is there a coaching program for staff who are finding it difficult? Are we training new staff? Are we celebrating success and finding new ways to invigorate the processes?

12. What is the ongoing continual improvement process? Who owns it? Who is funding it? Who is monitoring their accountability? What are we measuring? What are the improvement goals and who is setting them?

13. What are the succession plans? Who will be the next owners and stewards of ITIL?

14. What is the next phase or project? When will it be?

This is not an exhaustive list, just suggestions. Check the *Owning ITIL* webpage at www.itskeptic.org/owningitil to see if we have grown or revised this list, and to provide your own feedback so we can.

14 questions for an

ITIL environment

health check

1. Who owns the relationship with each customer? Are all customers owned?

2. What service catalogue do customers see? Users? IT staff? (See p90)

3. How do users request a new service or a change to how they get the service? How is that provisioned?

4. When did you last celebrate good performance or a goal met?

5. What person owns each process?

6. What accountability do people have for process compliance? How is it measured? Rewarded?

7. Is the service performance benchmarked and reviewed regularly? What is the process to act on unacceptable results of that review?

8. What training and coaching are new staff given? Check it includes work procedures. Do existing staff get updates and refreshers?

9. What has improved in the last year? How can you tell?

10. How is customer satisfaction tracking? How is it measured? How often?

11. How is user satisfaction tracking? (Not the same thing. Customers pay. Users use.)

12. How do you review processes and procedures? Who is involved? How often?

13. When was the last priority 1 incident?

14. What is the data quality of reports, especially service levels? What can't you report on?

This is not an exhaustive list, just suggestions. Check the *Owning ITIL* webpage at www.itskeptic.org/owningitil to see if we have grown or revised this list, and to provide your own feedback so we can.

Index

About the author:

The IT Skeptic is the pseudonym of Rob England, an IT consultant and commentator. Although he works around the ITIL industry, he is self-employed and his future is not dependant on ITIL – he has nothing to sell you but the ideas in this book.

He has twenty years experience mapping business requirements to IT solutions, ten of them in service management. (Some readers will be relieved to learn that this book reveals what "service management" means). He is active in the itSMF (the professional body for ITIL). He is the author of a popular blog www.itskeptic.org, a humorous book *Introduction to Real ITSM*, and a number of internet articles taking a critical look at IT's absurdities, especially those relating to ITIL. He is also a paid-up Skeptic. He lives with his wife and son in a small house in a small village in a small country far away.

The Worst of the IT Skeptic

A compilation of writings from the first three years of the IT Skeptic so that you can conveniently read the wickedest wackiest wittiest posts of your favourite IT bombast.

This material is delivered to you in a special media presentation technology known as a "book": affordable, flexible, robust, light, compact, wireless, with a remarkably low power consumption, zero boot time, integral bookmarking and annotation functions, permitted on airplanes even during takeoff and landing, and readable in daylight.

See www.itskeptic.org/worst

Working in IT

Our career, our profession. This book is a collection of Rob's writing about IT people (including some unpublished material): collated, edited and improved. It reflects the author's own experiences and inspirations, it does not set out to be a comprehensive survey of the topics. Here you will find ideas and inspiration to think about your own career and the careers of those who work for you, and to make a difference in both.

See www.itskeptic.org/working

He Tangata

IT is the people.

To be published in 2009. See www.itskeptic.org/hetangata

2675495

Made in the USA